ASK SEW NEWS

150 SEWING ANSWERS

ASK SEW NEWS

Cindy Kacynski: *Book Editor*

Elizabeth Brkich: *Book Design*

Pudik Art Studios Inc.: *Book Production*

Staff At PJS Publications Inc.:

Linda Turner Griepentrog: *SEW NEWS Editor*

Darlene Luther: *SEW NEWS Art Director*

Janet Timian: *SEW NEWS Circulation Manager*

Sylvia Miller: *Publications Director*

Del Rusher: *Vice President/Creative Woman's Group Publisher*

Jerry R. Constantino: *President*

PJS Publications Inc.
News Plaza, Peoria, IL 61656

Copyright© 1992
ISBN 0-9621148-7-1

TABLE OF CONTENTS

FOREWARD

Sewing has been my hobby and vocation for more than half my life. I can't imagine my world without this wonderful, creative outlet. One of the most exciting things about sewing is that the more you sew, the more you learn. And the more new things you try, the more questions you're bound to have. I know that's true in my case. Besides solving my own sewing challenges, I've had the opportunity to address the questions of SEW NEWS readers in my monthly column, "Sewing Q&A." I'm always surprised at the diversity of the questions, as well as those which fashion-sewers seem to have in common as a group. At least one question on fitting makes its way to my desk each month. However, the subjects brought to my attention are as different as the crop of readers who write to me.

In answering these questions, I've shared my personal techniques as well as tried-and-true methods that have stood the test of time. Occasionally, a question appears which has me stumped. Then I consult other sewing experts for the answers—and learn something new to share with the SEW NEWS readers.

Now, thanks to the editors of SEW NEWS, 150 of the most common (and not-so-common) sewing questions have been compiled into this easy-to-use answer book. Organized into sensible sections, such as "Alterations/Fitting," "Fabrics" and "Pressing," the book also offers an extensive index for quick reference. Whatever the subject of your sewing question, you'll find it quickly and easily to solve your sewing dilemma with confidence. How nice to have the answers right at your fingertips!

Whether you're a beginner or seasoned fashion-sewer, you're bound to have a question or two or three...And I know you'll use this valuable reference again and again as you encounter new sewing challenges. When you need an answer fast, reach for ASK SEW NEWS first!

— Barbara Weiland
Columnist, Author, Editor

Q How can I minimize the shoulder and modify the armholes on extended-shoulder, dropped-armhole patterns?

A Since the modification you describe requires redrafting the shape of the sleeve cap, this change isn't recommended. It would be far easier and wiser to buy a pattern with the armhole shape you prefer. However, if you love all the other design features in a particular pattern, except for the armhole, try combining two patterns: Lay the pattern with the extended shoulder over a pattern with a shoulder and armhole you prefer, tracing the new armhole and underarm seam onto the original pattern (A). Use the sleeve pattern for the new armhole, rather than trying to change the original sleeve.

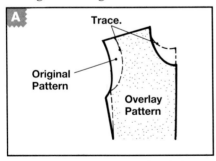

Trace.

Original Pattern

Overlay Pattern

If you try this method, be sure to test the change in muslin or pattern tracing cloth before cutting the actual garment.

Q How can I alter a blouse pattern for a larger bra cup size when using a dartless pattern?

A Simply follow these steps:
✂ Wearing a properly fitted bra, determine your bust point position by measuring from the center of your shoulder to your bust point, then from bust point to bust point (A).

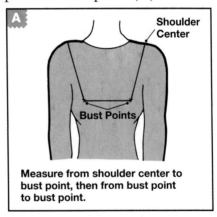

A

Shoulder Center

Bust Points

Measure from shoulder center to bust point, then from bust point to bust point.

Measure and mark the intersection of these two measurements on your blouse front pattern, remembering to divide the bust point-to-bust point measurement in half when measuring from the pattern center front (B, page 6).

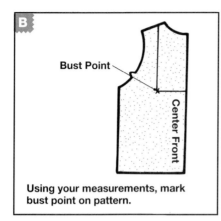

Using your measurements, mark bust point on pattern.

✂ From the bust point, draw three lines: Line A at a slightly downward angle to the side seam; Line B to the front armhole notch center; and Line C straight down to the waistline (or jacket or bodice lower edge) (C). *Note:* In general, Line A should be fairly high under the arm and drop at a slight angle. However, this will vary on individual figures. Test the pattern with the bustline dart alteration in muslin so you can adjust the dart placement to suit your taste and figure.

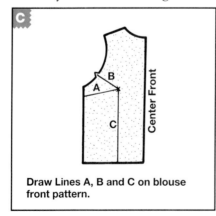

Draw Lines A, B and C on blouse front pattern.

✂ Slash the pattern on Line A *to, but not through,* the bust point and from the bottom of Line C through the bust point and along Line B, stopping just before the armhole edge. Place pattern tracing cloth or tissue paper under the slashed pattern.

✂ Spread the pattern along Line B-C the necessary amount—at Line C, approximately ½" for a C cup, ¾" for a D cup and 1¼" or more for larger sizes. As you spread the tissue, a bust dart will open up along Line A. Tape the adjusted pattern to the tracing cloth (D).

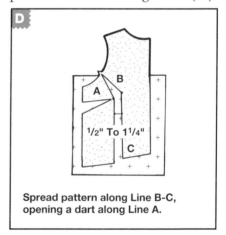

Spread pattern along Line B-C, opening a dart along Line A.

✂ Even the pattern lower edge on the added tracing cloth (E, page 7).

Note: The above adjustment will create extra bodice length needed to cover a fuller figure.

✂ Draw the dart foldline in the center of the newly formed dart area, stopping 1" to 2" from the bust point. *Note:* In

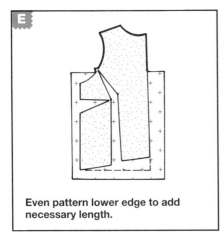

Even pattern lower edge to add necessary length.

general, fuller figures require a shorter line, less-full figures, a longer line. To determine the best foldline length for your figure, test first on a muslin.

✂ Draw dart stitching lines from the dart outer edges to the bust point (F).

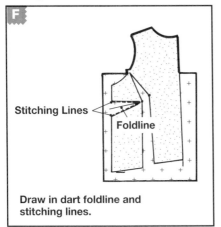

Stitching Lines

Foldline

Draw in dart foldline and stitching lines.

✂ Fold out the dart and draw in the outer dart point cutting line. Trim away the excess adjustment tissue.

✂ To take up the excess fullness created along the pattern lower edge, make a lengthwise dart from that edge to 1" to 2" below the bust point (G), determining the exact point on a muslin as noted above.

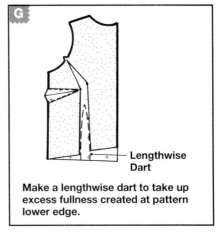

Lengthwise Dart

Make a lengthwise dart to take up excess fullness created at pattern lower edge.

Q **I'm rather petite with a generous C-cup bra size. How do I adjust jacket patterns so there's enough fabric to fit my curves? My jacket lapels never seem to lie smoothly.**

A Because patterns are made for the average 22-year-old figure with a B-cup bra size, you'll need to add darts to your jacket pattern to fit your more generous curves. To choose the correct pattern size, substitute your high bust measurement for your full bust measurement; the resulting size will fit your smaller frame in the shoulder, upper chest and neckline. Add the bustline darts described in Question No. 2 (page 5).

A jacket pattern with princess seaming is also an excellent option, because you can cut deeper seam allowances to allow room for your fuller cup size.

To make jacket lapels hug your fuller curves, tape each roll line:

✂ Cut a piece of ¼"-wide twill tape ⅜" shorter than the length of the roll line. *Note:* For fuller bust cup sizes, shorten the tape ½" instead of ⅜".

✂ Pin the twill tape inside the roll line (away from the lapel) at both ends. *Note:* The tape will be too short.

✂ Pin the remaining tape next to the roll line, distributing the lapel fullness evenly along the twill tape (A).

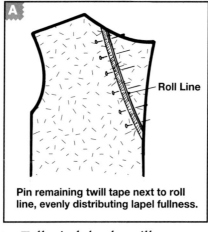

Pin remaining twill tape next to roll line, evenly distributing lapel fullness.

✂ Fell stitch both twill tape

edges to the jacket (B).

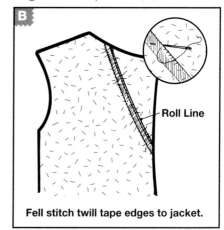

Roll Line

Fell stitch twill tape edges to jacket.

Q **4** **Help! How can I adjust dartless patterns for a small bust? The garments I sew have too much fabric in front, causing vertical wrinkles to form on blouses, dresses and jackets.**

A You should make a small bust adjustment to the front pattern piece *before* cutting out the garment. This involves taking a tuck from the pattern upper edge to the lower edge, making the bodice smaller through the bustline (A, page 9).

This will also make the front shoulder narrower and the waistline smaller, so you may need to adjust these areas back

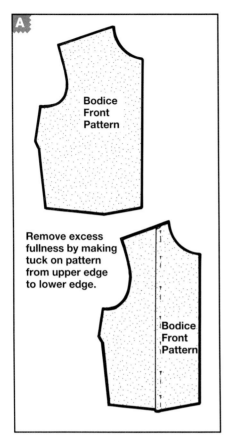

A

Bodice Front Pattern

Remove excess fullness by making tuck on pattern from upper edge to lower edge.

Bodice Front Pattern

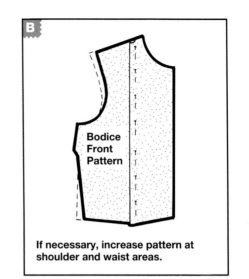

B

Bodice Front Pattern

If necessary, increase pattern at shoulder and waist areas.

to their original size after taking the tuck out for the bustline fullness (B)—unless you have narrower-than-average shoulders and a small waist which correspond to the above adjustment.

To determine how much fullness to remove, try on a garment you've sewn that has the wrinkles you describe and pin out (tuck) the extra fullness through the bustline. Use the tuck depth as a guide for the

paper pattern adjustment—assuming you're using the same size pattern as the one you used for the test garment. If you no longer have a "problem" garment or you've changed sizes, keep in mind it will be well worth your time to make a muslin to test the adjustment. Once you know how much smaller you are than the size you normally sew, you'll be able to adjust any pattern.

Just a word of caution concerning darts: Many people try to fit a small figure by taking deeper darts, not knowing that deeper darts only make room for a larger cup size! On patterns with darts, take a *narrower* dart and remove the excess fabric by taking in the front waistline (C, page 10).

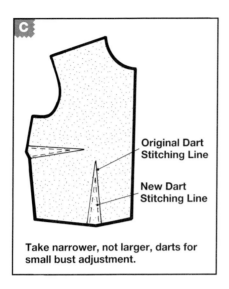

Original Dart
Stitching Line

New Dart
Stitching Line

Take narrower, not larger, darts for
small bust adjustment.

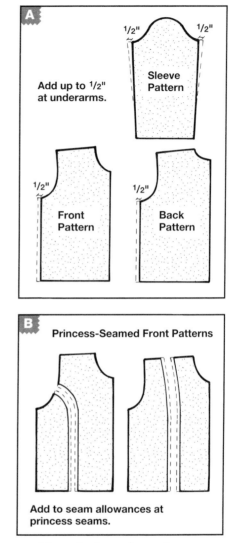

Add up to 1/2"
at underarms.

1/2"   1/2"

Sleeve
Pattern

1/2"   1/2"

Front
Pattern

Back
Pattern

B Princess-Seamed Front Patterns

Add to seam allowances at
princess seams.

Q How can I adjust a
pattern for a fuller
bust size without
adding darts? I don't want
to destroy the intended
design on more detailed
garments.

5

A Add as much as 2" of
extra bustline room by
adding ½" at garment
underarm seams (A). Creating
a strong shoulder line with
shoulder pads also helps minimize the bustline.

Another method for fitting a
fuller bustline is to choose patterns with princess seams and add
extra room at the seamlines (B).

Also, designs featuring
shoulder yokes with soft gathers or pleats just below the
shoulder are naturally roomier
in the bust, and it's easy to add
even more room by slashing
and spreading the pattern (C,
page 11).

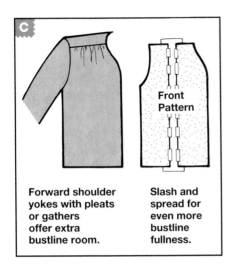

Forward shoulder yokes with pleats or gathers offer extra bustline room.

Front Pattern

Slash and spread for even more bustline fullness.

Q I love to sew, but the garments I make for myself are always too big through the shoulders and bust and show dimples and wrinkles in these areas. Based on my measurements, I buy a Misses size 6. How do I adjust patterns for a perfect fit?

A The reason your garments are always too large through the shoulders and bust is probably because the pattern you've chosen is too large to fit these areas of your body, and the wrinkles you described are a result of this size discrepancy.

First, take your measurements and be sure you have the correct pattern size: Measure the fullest part of your bustline and your high bust and compare the two measurements (A); if you find a difference of 2" or more, substitute the high bust for the bust measurement when choosing the pattern size. *Note:* This means choosing a smaller size that will fit your neckline and shoulder area better but will probably require a bustline adjustment.

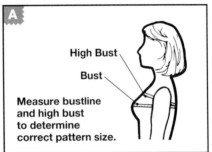

High Bust

Bust

Measure bustline and high bust to determine correct pattern size.

Purchase the smallest size pattern available and adjust the pattern through the shoulders, before cutting, for a better fit. To do this:

✂ Measure your front and back shoulder width and bust and compare with the pattern.

✂ If the difference is ½" or less, simply redraw the shoulder and armhole to eliminate the excess.

• Compare your front shoulder measurement to the width of the front shoulder on the pattern piece; this difference determines how much to narrow the shoulder.

• Narrow the shoulder width the amount needed and redraw the armhole using a curved ruler (B).

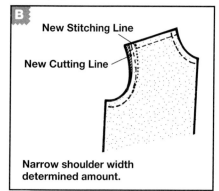

B

New Stitching Line

New Cutting Line

Narrow shoulder width determined amount.

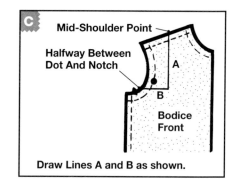

C

Mid-Shoulder Point

Halfway Between Dot And Notch

A

B

Bodice Front

Draw Lines A and B as shown.

• Make the same change on the back shoulder and armhole so the shoulder edges will meet at the seamline.

✄ If the difference is more than ½", remove excess by cutting and sliding the armhole area on the bodice.

• On the bodice front pattern, draw Line A parallel to the grainline from the center of the shoulder to halfway between the dot and the armhole notch.

• Draw Line B just above the armhole notch and perpendicular to Line A (C).

• Cut a wedge from the pattern along Lines A and B, then slide it in to narrow the shoulder the necessary amount; tape in place and redraw the shoulder and armhole cutting lines (D).

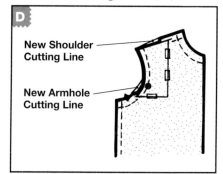

D

New Shoulder Cutting Line

New Armhole Cutting Line

• Make the same changes on the back pattern pieces.

✄ Using the adjusted pattern, continue following the pattern guidesheet.

Q **There's never enough room across the back of the clothes I sew, especially suit jackets, so I'm always uncomfortable when I wear them. How can I remedy this problem?**

7

A To make a broad back alteration and achieve a more comfortable fit in finished garments:

✂ Remove the stitching in the back armhole.

✂ Let out the jacket underarm seam ¼" to ⅜", tapering the extension back to the original side seamline.

✂ Reset the sleeve back in the armhole, letting it out ¼" to ⅜" at the notch and tapering the extension to the original seamline at the shoulder and underarm (A).

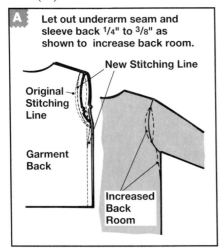

A Let out underarm seam and sleeve back 1/4" to 3/8" as shown to increase back room.

New Stitching Line

Original Stitching Line

Garment Back

Increased Back Room

If you find this small amount of change corrects the problem, continue to make this adjustment to all your patterns before cutting. However, if you would be more comfortable with even more room across the back, see Question No. 8 below.

Q **I have a very broad back and need some fitting advice. How can I alter jacket patterns to accommodate this area and achieve a more comfortable fit?**

8

A Make the following adjustment to your garment back patterns before cutting:

✂ Draw Line A from the shoulder seam center to the pattern lower edge, parallel to the grainline. Draw Line B from the armhole center to Line A, perpendicular to Line A. Draw Line C 1" below the armhole lower edge, parallel to Line B (A, page 14).

✂ Cut out the section between Lines B and C as shown and slide it, adding up to 1" for smaller sizes and up to 1½" for larger sizes (16 or larger). Tape the adjusted pattern area to a

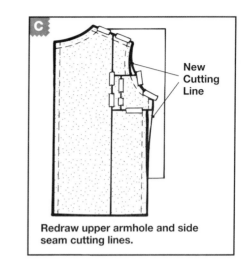

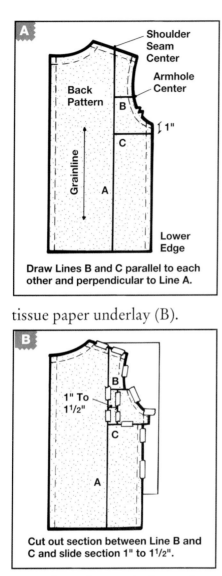

A

Shoulder Seam Center

Armhole Center

Back Pattern

B

1"

C

Grainline

A

Lower Edge

Draw Lines B and C parallel to each other and perpendicular to Line A.

tissue paper underlay (B).

B

B

1" To 1½"

C

A

Cut out section between Line B and C and slide section 1" to 1½".

✂ Redraw the armhole cutting line between the shoulder and the adjusted section upper corner, using a French curve. Taper the side seam from the adjusted section lower edge to the garment back lower edge (C). Trim away the excess tissue on the new cutting lines.

C

New Cutting Line

Redraw upper armhole and side seam cutting lines.

9

Q How can I alter the shoulder width on blouses and dresses with cut-on sleeves?

A You must first "separate" the sleeve from the bodice.
✂ Draw Line A parallel to the grainline, extending it from the shoulder (approximately 4" from the neckline) to just below the underarm curve. Draw Line B perpendicular to the grainline to meet the lower end of Line A (A, page 15). Cut the pattern apart on these lines.
✂ For broad shoulders, spread the pattern at the shoulder seam the necessary amount. Place tissue paper underneath and tape it in place; blend the cutting and stitching lines at

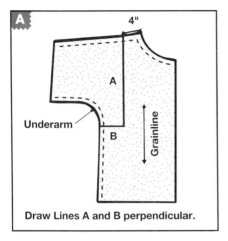

Draw Lines A and B perpendicular.

the underarm and shoulder seams (B). Check the new sleeve length and adjust as necessary.

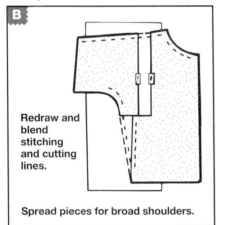

Redraw and blend stitching and cutting lines.

Spread pieces for broad shoulders.

✂ For narrow shoulders, overlap the pattern pieces the amount needed. Place tissue paper underneath and tape it in place; blend the cutting and stitching lines at the underarm and shoulder seams (C). Check the new sleeve length and adjust as necessary.

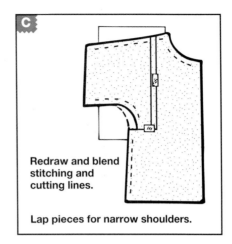

Redraw and blend stitching and cutting lines.

Lap pieces for narrow shoulders.

Remember to repeat any adjustments on the remaining bodice/sleeve pattern pieces.

Q **With middle age, my upper arms have increased in size, and set-in sleeves are always too tight. How can I adjust my patterns for a better fit in this area?**

10

A This is not an uncommon problem. To make the adjustment:
✂ Measure the fullest part of the upper arm and add the minimum wearing ease (shown in the following chart) for the type of garment you're making (A, page 16).
✂ Compare this measurement to the pattern measurement at the upper arm (seamline to

A

GARMENT	MIN. UPPER ARM EASE
BLOUSE	1½" TO 2½"
DRESS; JUMPSUIT	1½" TO 2½"
LINED JACKET	3" TO 4½"
UNLINED JACKET	3" TO 4"
COAT	4" TO 5½"

seamline) to determine the amount of change needed (B).

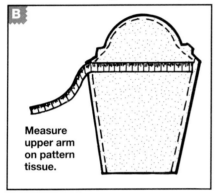

B

Measure upper arm on pattern tissue.

✂ Draw Line A down the center of the sleeve parallel to the grainline. Draw Line B perpendicular to Line A from underarm to underarm (C).
✂ Cut the pattern on Lines A and B, cutting up to but *not through* the edges, and spread

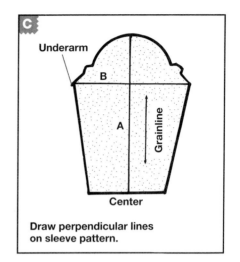

C

Underarm

B

A

Grainline

Center

Draw perpendicular lines on sleeve pattern.

at the center the amount determined above; redraw the original sleeve cap shape if the change is more than 1" (D).

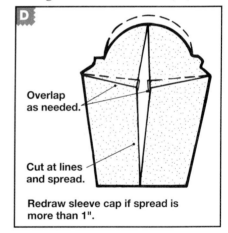

D

Overlap as needed.

Cut at lines and spread.

Redraw sleeve cap if spread is more than 1".

Q I love surplice-wrap bodices on blouses and dresses, but they tend to gap on me. Can you recommend how to fit this style more closely so I don't have to use a safety pin to keep it closed?

11

A For a smooth, non-gapping fit in wrap-front designs, use woven tape in the front neckline seam allowance to prevent stretching and make the garment hug your curves.

✂ Measure the neckline seamline on the pattern front and cut a piece of ¼"-wide twill tape or stay tape the same length (A).

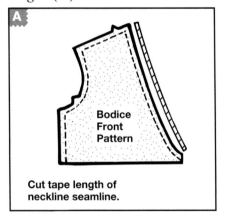

Cut tape length of neckline seamline.

✂ On the wrong side of the bodice front, pin one end of the tape at the neckline/shoulder, centering it over the stitching line; pin the other end to the bodice at the waistline, shortening the tape ¼" for small bustlines, ⅜" for medium bustlines and ½" for full bustlines. Pin the tape in place, distributing the fullness along the seamline. Stitch in place just inside the neckline seamline (B).

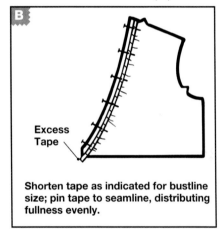

Excess Tape

Shorten tape as indicated for bustline size; pin tape to seamline, distributing fullness evenly.

This same technique can be used to stay the roll line of a jacket to prevent lapel gapping (see Question No. 3, page 7) and to stabilize slant pockets in trouser styles for a smoother fit.

Q The blouses I've sewn recently seem to creep up in the front and hang down in the back, gapping at the neckline. How can I adjust the pattern to correct this problem?

12

A Sometimes this happens because the blouse is not full enough through the bustline, so it naturally shifts up on your body to allow room for your fullness. It can also be due to how the front and back pattern pieces are shaped in comparison to your own front and back shape. Posture also plays a role. To determine if the pattern pieces deviate from your body measurements:

✂ Have a friend measure from the base of your neck at the shoulder to your waistline, straight down your front and straight down your back (A).

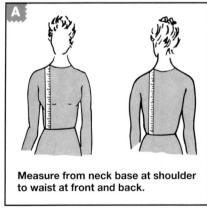

Measure from neck base at shoulder to waist at front and back.

Record these measurements. ✂ Compare these measurements to the pattern pieces in the same locations. Often the front and back pattern pieces measure the same but you do not. Usually the back measurement is slightly larger than the front. If this is the case, adjust the pattern, then reshape the bodice front and back:

• Calculate the difference between your front and back body measurements. *Note:* Even a ⅛" difference will affect the fit, and the difference can be as much as ¾".

• Add the difference (excess) to the bodice back shoulder seam and subtract it from the bodice front shoulder seam (B).

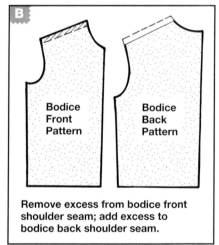

Bodice Front Pattern

Bodice Back Pattern

Remove excess from bodice front shoulder seam; add excess to bodice back shoulder seam.

• Reshape the bodice front by adding the difference (excess) to the neckline and removing it from the armhole; do the reverse on the bodice back (C).

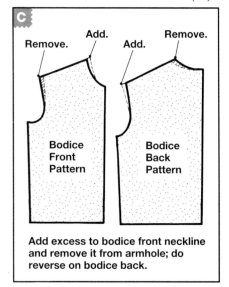

Add excess to bodice front neckline and remove it from armhole; do reverse on bodice back.

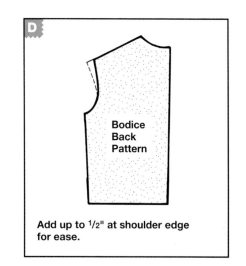

Add up to 1/2" at shoulder edge for ease.

For an obviously rounded upper back, you can achieve a better fit by adding ease to the back shoulder seam if the pattern's back shoulder edge isn't already longer than the front shoulder edge. Add up to an additional ½" at the shoulder edge on the bodice back *only* (D).

Note: Be sure to adjust the facings to match the changes you've made on the bodice front and back.

Q **13** **I have several knit sweaters that need adjustment. How can I take them in at the shoulders, arms and sides without using a serger?**

A Although sergers are ideal for altering sweaters, you can make these changes on your conventional machine.

✂ Carefully remove the sleeves and set them aside. If the seam edges ravel easily, treat them sparingly with seam sealant.

✂ Adjust the fit through the shoulder seams, tapering the adjustment to nothing at the neckline.

✂ Permanently stitch the new shoulder seam in a close straight stitch or a tiny zigzag, catching a piece of seam or twill tape in the stitching to prevent stretching. *Note:* Also check your machine's instruction manual for other appropriate stitches for sweater knits.

✄ Stitch again close to the first stitching and trim close to the tape's edge (A).

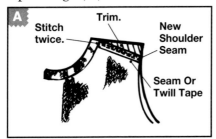

Stitch twice.

Trim.

New Shoulder Seam

Seam Or Twill Tape

✄ Repeat this process for the side seams, omitting the seam tape.

✄ Set the sleeves into the adjusted sweater as usual, using easestitching to fit them into the armholes.

✄ Doublestitch and trim the armhole seams as explained for the shoulder seam.

Q **I have osteoporosis and am difficult to fit. Because sweaters are so fashionable and comfortable for people with my figure problem, I'd like to know how to alter a pattern for a sweater knit. Will sweater knits take a dart like the one I add at the**

14

back neckline when I make pattern alterations for my rounded back?

A Heavy sweater knits with minimal stretch are more suitable for dart-fitting than stretchy ones. However, you can achieve the benefits of a dart without even stitching one, using the right combination of sweater knit fabric and garment styling:

✄ Alter your pattern as usual for rounded back adjustments (A).

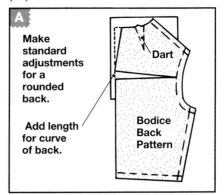

Make standard adjustments for a rounded back.

Dart

Add length for curve of back.

Bodice Back Pattern

✄ Choose a stretchy sweater knit and a design with simple bodice styling featuring a collar and/or facing.

✄ Instead of stitching the dart, ease the additional fullness to fit the facing or collar (B, page 21).

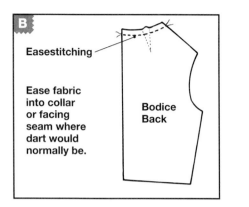

Easestitching

Ease fabric into collar or facing seam where dart would normally be.

Bodice Back

wearing ease through the hipline. While you don't need quite that much ease through the tummy and upper hip, you should be able to get at least one thumb into the waistband comfortably. If you can't, start fitting your skirts with more room in these areas. Also note that very stiff fabrics with little or no give will naturally hike up a little more than softer fabrics, even when they fit properly.

Q **Why do certain skirts ride up my midriff when I sit down? I haven't been able to determine whether it's the style, fit or some other cause.**

15

A The skirts may be too tight through the upper hip, across the tummy or in the hip—or in all three areas. When you sit down, everything spreads a little; that's one reason you need ease in fitted garments. Because most garments are a little wider below the hipline, they naturally hike up to accommodate your "wider" frame when you sit down.

In fitted skirt styles, you should be able to "pinch an inch" of extra fabric at the fullest part of your hips; that means you have at least 2" of

Q **My hips are about 10" larger than my waist and I have difficulty fitting my hip contour. The hem allowance on the sides is always about 1" narrower than the hem allowance in the front and back. How can I correct this problem?**

16

A The difference between your waist and hip measurements creates a larger-than-average curve. And because more fabric is required to cover a curve than a straight line, the sides of your pattern aren't long enough to cover the curve. That's why the hem allowance varies. The following unconventional adjustment might

work—try it on a muslin fitting shell first:

✂ Cut and sew a straight, fitted skirt pattern from muslin, adding approximately 1" at the waistline on the side seams. Try it on to test the fit.

✂ On the front and back pattern pieces, draw Line A 2" to 3" below the hipline and perpendicular to the grainline. Draw Line B parallel to the grainline between the dart and side seam (A).

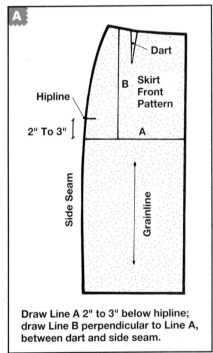

Draw Line A 2" to 3" below hipline; draw Line B perpendicular to Line A, between dart and side seam.

✂ Cut the pattern pieces apart on the lines and slide the hip section up 1". Tape the pieces together and add tissue paper to fill the resulting gap. Use a curved ruler to blend the

stitching line back to normal at the center front (B).

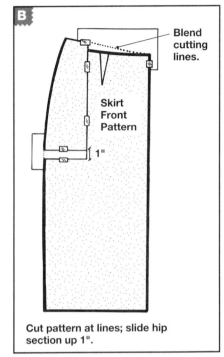

Cut pattern at lines; slide hip section up 1".

✂ To make sure you're cutting the skirt with at least 2" of ease at the fullest part of your hip, measure from the waist to the fullest point of your hip. Measure the pattern pieces in that location to check for ease, adding as necessary.

When you've allowed enough length in the side seams to cover your curve, the hem allowance available should be approximately the same width all around. On a straight skirt, that means the hem will be turned on the *straight* grain as it should be.

If this adjustment solves your problem, you'll want to make it on pants patterns as well.

Q **When trying on my evenly hemmed basic straight, fitted skirts, the back hangs or sags noticeably. How can I correct this problem?**

17

A This fairly common problem is usually caused by a flat derriere which doesn't properly fill out the back skirt curve, causing the extra fabric to sag and hang lower in back than in front. To determine if this is the case for you, check the skirt from the side view. Do the side seams swing forward? Does the skirt back touch or come close to the back of your legs (A)?

A

A flat derriere will cause side seams to swing forward and back hem to fall close to legs.

If so, you can correct the hang of the skirt by lowering the waistband across the center back waistline. To do so:

✂ Remove the waistband across the back between the side seams.

✂ Try on the skirt and pull it up in back until the side seams hang straight and the skirt is balanced on your body. Mark the new waistline at the center back (B).

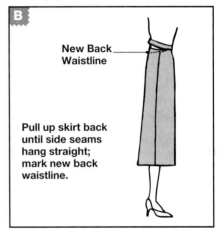

B

New Back Waistline

Pull up skirt back until side seams hang straight; mark new back waistline.

✂ Remove the center back zipper, if applicable; reapply it lower in the seam according to the new back waistline location.

✂ Trim the excess fabric, then restitch the waistband at the new center back location, tapering back to the original waistline location at the side seams.

✂ Note the amount you lowered the waistband for future reference when making the same adjustment on other skirts you sew.

Q Can you explain how to add a "tummy control" panel to my slacks?

18

A Also called a "front stay," a tummy control panel can be cut from a firmly woven cotton blend for light control or from nylon/Lycra® power net fabric for firm control.

The front stay is actually an extension of the pocket, caught in the center front seam. To make a front stay pattern:
✂ Pin out the darts or pleats in the pants front pattern.
✂ Position and pin the pocket pattern on the pants front pattern; extend the pocket to the center front in a gentle curve for the front stay pattern, with the stay lower edge ¼" to ½" below the fly front zipper opening (A).
✂ Trace and cut the front stay pattern from pattern tracing cloth or tissue paper (B); cut two from the fabric you've chosen.
✂ Sew the darts or tucks in the pants front. Right sides together, pin then stitch the front

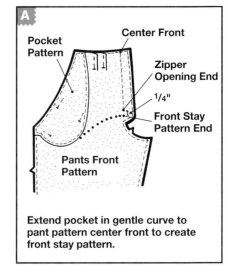

A

Pocket Pattern

Center Front

Zipper Opening End

¼"

Front Stay Pattern End

Pants Front Pattern

Extend pocket in gentle curve to pant pattern center front to create front stay pattern.

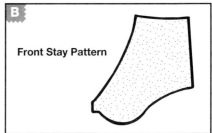

B

Front Stay Pattern

stays to the pants pocket edges (C).

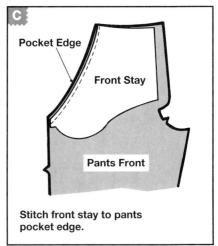

C

Pocket Edge

Front Stay

Pants Front

Stitch front stay to pants pocket edge.

✂ Trim the seams, turn the front stays and pants fronts wrong sides together, press and edgestitch along the pocket edges only (D).

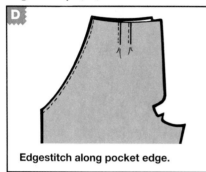

Edgestitch along pocket edge.

✂ Pin and stitch each pants side front/pocket to the respective front stay, keeping the stitching free from the pants fronts (E).

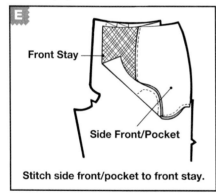

Front Stay

Side Front/Pocket

Stitch side front/pocket to front stay.

✂ Machine baste each front stay's front edge to the pants center front (F), then complete the pants construction following the pattern guidesheet.

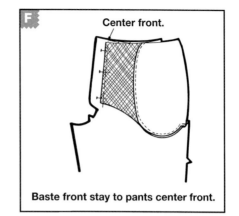

Center front.

Baste front stay to pants center front.

Q **19** **What is the general rule to follow when choosing pant leg widths? I don't have the figure to wear the current, tapered-to-fit styles.**

A A flattering and always "safe" in-fashion width around the pant lower edge is 20" to 22".

To adjust too-narrow patterns, determine how much you need to add to each leg, divide by two and add this amount equally to the inseam and the side seam at the hem edge. Draw new cutting lines, tapering from just below the full hip on the side seam and just above the knee on the inseam (A, page 26).

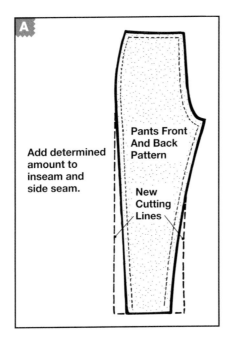

Add determined amount to inseam and side seam.

Pants Front And Back Pattern

New Cutting Lines

the waistband pattern. *Note:* This might require easing the waistline of the pants onto the waistband.

✂ For a total increase of 1½", cut the pant adding ⅜" at each waistline side seam, tapering to nothing at the full hip where the pant pattern fits you (A), then add 1½" to your waist-band pattern. Your side seam will not be as curved as the original because *your* "curve" is straighter than the pattern.

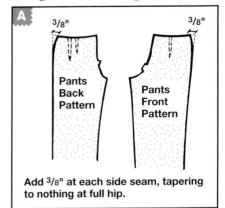

3/8"   3/8"

Pants Back Pattern   Pants Front Pattern

Add ⅜" at each side seam, tapering to nothing at full hip.

Q **How can I alter a pant pattern waist-line? My pattern size fits everywhere except in the waist area where I need an additional 1" to 1½" for a comfortable fit.**

20

A You're on the right track by selecting a pant pattern that fits through the hipline, and adjusting the waistline is easy. You have two options:
✂ Eliminate the front and back darts or stitch narrower darts to acquire extra room through the waistline, then add the amount adjusted in the darts to

21 **Q** **Please help! How can I prevent the pants I make from sweatshirt fleece from bagging at the knees?**

A First, be sure to use a sweatshirt fleece that has some built-in stretch recovery—cotton with a small Lycra® content would be perfect.

Also, consider stabilizing the areas prone to bagging—for example, knees and elbows. To do this, cut a large patch of a stable (non-stretch) fusible interfacing and apply it to the wrong side of the knee or elbow areas before stitching the seams, pinking the interfacing edges that won't be included in the seams so sharp edges won't show on the garment right side (A). *Note:* Be sure to follow the manufacturer's instructions for fusing and test first on a fabric scrap.

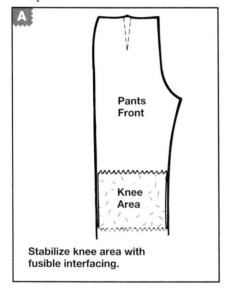

Stabilize knee area with fusible interfacing.

22 Q **I have a flat derriere and have trouble fitting pants. Can you help?**

A First, lower the waistband in back (see Question No. 17 on page 23). Using the following adjustment, you'll be able to rescue many ill-fitting pants you already own:

✂ Try on the pants and "guesstimate" how much extra fabric you have across the back thigh, just under the derriere, by pinching out the excess. Remove the pants and turn them inside out.

✂ Remove the crotch curve stitching for 2" to 3" on each side of the inseam (A).

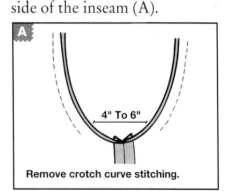

4" To 6"

Remove crotch curve stitching.

✂ Remove the stitching in the inseams from the crotch to a point halfway between the knee and crotch.

✂ Remove the amount of excess fabric you determined earlier by taking a deeper seam allowance in the *back inseams only*, tapering the adjustment to nothing; machine baste the new inseams (B), then the crotch curve.

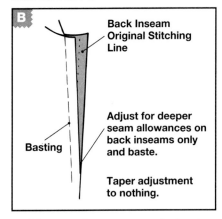

Try on the pants and check the fit. Make any necessary adjustments, taking in or letting out the back inseam allowance as necessary. Permanently stitch the inseams and crotch curve; remove the basting and trim the seam allowances to an even width.

This adjustment combined with lowering the back waistline may make the back crotch curve fit too snugly. If so, stitch a ¼" deeper curve in the back as shown (C). Trim the new seam to ¼" and try on the pants. If they're still too tight, stitch another ¼" deeper, trim and try on again.

Continue lowering the sitting room in this manner until the back crotch curve is comfortable in both standing and sitting positions. Reinforce the

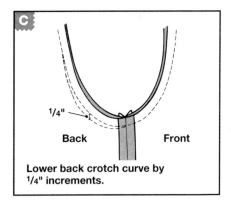

final seam with a second row of stitching ⅛" from the seamline.

23 **Q** **What type of adjustments can I make on patterns to accommodate large thighs?**

A To adjust pant patterns for full thighs, you may need to make the adjustment in two areas or only one: On some figures, the fullness is in the outer thigh, which means you'll need to let the side seam out from the hip down; other figures require extra room in the side seam *and* the inseam. The easiest way to solve the latter problem is to cut larger seam allowances in both areas, then fit as you sew. When cutting your next pair of pants:

✄ Cut 1"-wide side seams.
✄ Cut 2"-wide inseam seam allowances through the crotch

curve, then blend to ⅝" above the knee (A).

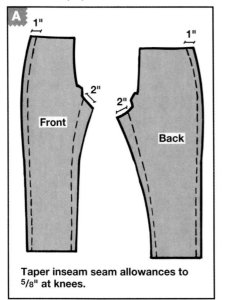

Taper inseam seam allowances to ⁵/₈" at knees.

✂ Baste the pants together, try on and adjust the inseam and side seams as necessary to allow for a better fit.

Unfortunately, trial and error is generally the best way to achieve a better fit through the thighs. Weight fluctuations and fashion design changes affect the amount of change you'll need to make, so just make it a habit to cut wider seams and fit as you sew.

Q **24** How can I choose the correct pattern size? I purchase a size 8 in ready-to-wear, but can't get into a size 10 straight skirt pattern. A size 14 fits me in the hips but is much too large in the waist. Help!

A You're definitely not alone! Most of us are victims of vanity sizing in ready-to-wear. It seems the more expensive the item, the smaller the size you wear—and if these sizes have any relationship to your pattern size, it's purely coincidental.

To determine your skirt/pant pattern size, measure your waistline, then your hipline at the fullest point (usually somewhere between 7" and 9" from the waistline). *Note:* Be sure you're measuring your hip and *not* your upper thigh.

For pants and fitted skirts, use the full hipline measurement to choose your pattern size. To adjust the waistline to fit:

✂ Wrong sides together, pin-fit the side seams, adjusting them to fit your curve from the hipline up to the waistline (A, page 30) . This is the best way to perfectly fit your hip curve—which often doesn't match the pattern curve.

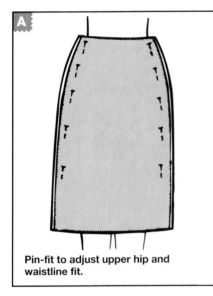

Pin-fit to adjust upper hip and waistline fit.

✂ Use an air- or water-soluble marker to mark the new stitching line on the fabric wrong side (B).

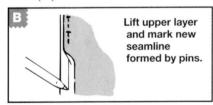

Lift upper layer and mark new seamline formed by pins.

✂ For fuller skirts, you can buy the pattern according to your waistline measurement, using excess fullness (design ease) as wearing ease.

25

Q How should personal body measurements compare to pattern measurements? For example, if my bust measures 38" and I buy a pattern to fit that measurement, what should the actual pattern measure in the same area?

A Your question relates to ease. If the pattern matched your measurement, you would find it difficult to impossible to get into the garment, let alone move in it because it would fit skin-tight (blue jeans, swimwear and bodywear might be exceptions).

The extra room built into a pattern is called ease. Most garments have at least minimum ease, called wearing ease. Many also have design ease, extra room beyond wearing ease to make the garment look and fit the way the designer intended it to look.

For fitted garments, you will need minimum wearing ease: 2½" to 3" in the bust; 2" through the full hipline; 1" in the waistline; and 1½" in the upper arm. Wearing ease is actually personal preference.

Note: For additional guidance while sewing, check the pattern for the finished width measurement, which is generally indicated on the pattern tissue at the bust or hip point.

Q 26 **I want to alter sport coats and suit jackets for my elderly father who is confined to a wheelchair. How can I modify the shape of too-long lapels that gap? Would it be better to make new jackets rather than altering old ones?**

A Jackets for the wheelchair-bound should be cut off at seat level and enlarged through the hipline by adjusting the hemline and letting out the side seams as much as possible (A).

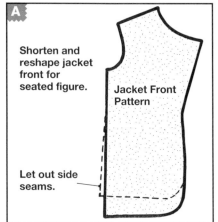

Shorten and reshape jacket front for seated figure.

Jacket Front Pattern

Let out side seams.

Adjusting jacket lapels is another story. Making a new jacket is the only option,

because the problem must be eliminated *before* the jacket is cut out by slashing and overlapping the lapel pattern in three places to shorten it. Wearing a *finished* jacket unbuttoned is really the only easy option to improve its lapels' appearance.

If you opt to make a jacket, take your father's measurements while he's seated in the wheelchair and learn to adapt a standard pattern for the shape of his seated figure. Making a muslin is an excellent idea in this case.

Q 27 **The coats I've sewn never lie flat against my body—they tend to hang open. What am I doing wrong?**

A You're probably not doing anything wrong—your pattern just needs a simple adjustment. Adding "walking ease" may seem strange, but you'll be thrilled with the results. Here's how to add it:

✂ Pin the coat front pattern to the fabric, allowing extra room along the center front seamline so you can add 2½" to the lower edge of a mid-calf-length coat, 2" to a knee-length coat and 1½" to a hip-length coat, tapering to nothing at the waist area (A).

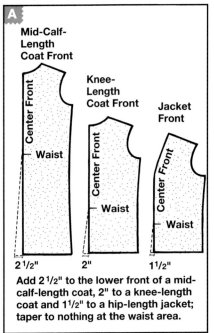

Add 2½" to the lower front of a mid-calf-length coat, 2" to a knee-length coat and 1½" to a hip-length jacket; taper to nothing at the waist area.

Note: This technique will not work on striped, plaid or other fabrics with a very noticeable pattern or grain.

Q Can you explain a simple way to lower or reduce the size of the leg openings and add to the seat of bathing suits for more coverage?

A The easiest technique for making the changes you've noted is the overlay method, using two pat-terns designed for fabrics with similar stretch:

✂ Choose a suit pattern with a comfortable leg and seat fit and trace the bottom half (front and back) on pattern tracing cloth (A).

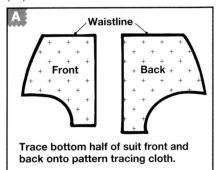

Trace bottom half of suit front and back onto pattern tracing cloth.

✂ Place this new pattern under the pattern you want to alter, matching centers and waistline marks; pin together to create a new suit pattern (B).

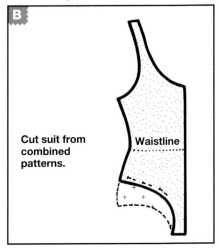

Cut suit from combined patterns.

This technique is easier than trying to lower the leg opening and cutting lines, which reduces the leg opening and

28

requires a change in the side seam fit and shape.

 I've recently started sewing for others. Can you guide me in establishing rates for common alterations and adjustments and prices for complete garments?

Establishing dressmaking/alteration rates and prices is an individual decision based on many factors. Your geographical area, the degree of difficulty of the project/garment, your skill level and the needs of your clientele and prospective clientele are all key considerations.

If you're offering services already widely available, pricing must be competitive. Customers will pay higher prices for specialized services not available elsewhere.

Perhaps your major consideration should be based on how much you plan to put into your dressmaking business. If you're only interested in making a little money for extras, your prices may be set lower than your competitors'. If supplementing the family budget is a high priority, your pricing should be based on a fair hourly wage—at least what you would expect to receive working outside the home. And while you may have year-end tax-deductible expenses, don't forget you're also liable for taxes on your dressmaking income, so factor this into pricing accordingly.

Q **I have a recurring problem with zipper insertion: I can't top-stitch around the zipper pull without ending up with crooked stitching in this area. I know I can use a longer zipper than the pattern suggests so the slider extends above the garment edge, then cut away the excess later, but how do I solve this problem when I can't buy a longer zipper than the size required—a 22" zipper in a dress back, for example?**

30

A To overcome the stitching bump around the zipper pull with ease:
✄ Baste the zipper in place with the zipper pull extending *above* the zipper slide top (A).

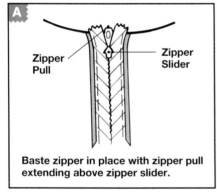

Baste zipper in place with zipper pull extending above zipper slider.

✄ For a lapped zipper:
• Topstitch across the zipper lower edge and toward the zipper upper edge, stopping stitching 1" from the zipper slider and leaving the needle in the fabric (B).

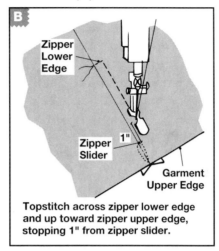

Topstitch across zipper lower edge and up toward zipper upper edge, stopping 1" from zipper slider.

• Lift the presser foot, then reach underneath and, through the fabric, push the pull tab away from you, maneuvering it to unzip the zipper until the tab is about 1" behind the zipper foot. Lower the zipper foot and complete the topstitching (C).

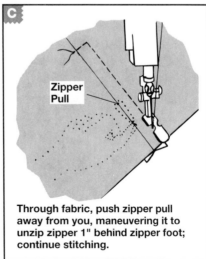

Through fabric, push zipper pull away from you, maneuvering it to unzip zipper 1" behind zipper foot; continue stitching.

• Pull the threads through to the garment wrong side at the zipper lower edge and tie them off. Remove the basting.

✂ For a centered application, you'll topstitch in two steps:

• Topstitch across the zipper lower edge and toward the zipper upper edge on one side, stopping the stitching 1" from the zipper pull and leaving the needle in the fabric (refer back to Illustration B on page 35).

• Lift the presser foot, then reach underneath and, through the fabric, push the pull tab away from you, maneuvering it to unzip the zipper until the tab is about 1" behind the zipper foot (refer back to Illustration C on page 35).

• Lower the zipper foot and complete the topstitching on that side only.

• Beginning at the zipper lower edge, stitch the unstitched side as instructed above (D).

• Pull the threads through to the garment wrong side at the zipper lower edge and tie them off. Remove the basting.

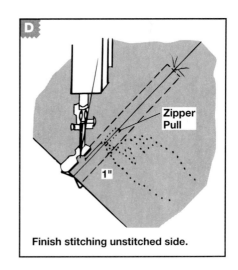

Finish stitching unstitched side.

31 *Q* **Are any special techniques required for stitching hook-and-loop tape, such as Velcro® in place?**

A For the best results, follow these tips:

✂ Angle the tape corners to eliminate sharp points.

✂ Use gluestick to position the tape.

✂ Use a size 14 or 16 sewing machine needle.

✂ Sew the tape very close to the edge with a stitch length of 8 to 10 stitches per inch (2.5mm to 3mm long).

✂ When sewing a strip, start near the center of one long edge and stitch around the tape, overlapping stitches at the beginning and end (A).

Secure hook-and-loop fastener strips by stitching close to edges and overlapping beginning and ending stitches.

✂ When sewing a circle, stitch in a triangle or square shape (B).

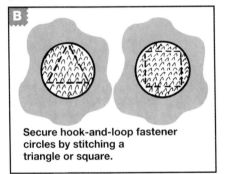

Secure hook-and-loop fastener circles by stitching a triangle or square.

Q I like a lapped zipper in dresses with center back openings. Is there an easy way to finish the neckline facing without too much bulk at the upper edge?

32

A This bulk-eliminating technique should work perfectly:

✂ Prepare the facing first: Press under 1" at the center back of the *left* facing and ⅝" on the *right* facing (A).

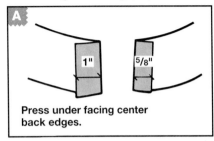

Press under facing center back edges.

✂ Press to the garment right side ⅝" on the *left* edge of the zipper opening and ½" on the *right* edge (B). Right sides together, pin and stitch the facings to the neckline; trim and grade the seam and turn the garment right side out.

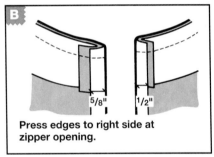

Press edges to right side at zipper opening.

✂ Press under ½" on the zipper opening *underlap* and ⅝" on the overlap.
✂ Hand-baste or use basting tape to position and hold the underlap in place along the zipper teeth; edgestitch (C, page 38). Zip the zipper.

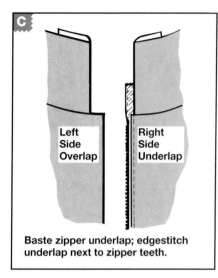

Baste zipper underlap; edgestitch underlap next to zipper teeth.

✂ Apply basting tape to the overlap edge wrong side and adhere it to cover the underlap (D).

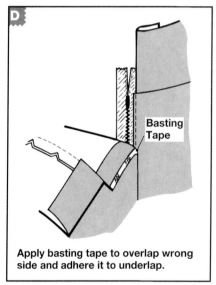

Apply basting tape to overlap wrong side and adhere it to underlap.

✂ Pin or hand-baste the zipper tape in place through all layers; topstitch approximately ½" from the overlap fold (E).

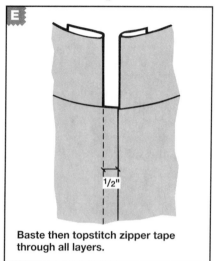

1/2"

Baste then topstitch zipper tape through all layers.

✂ Turn the facings to the inside and slipstitch the facing finished edges to the zipper tape (F).

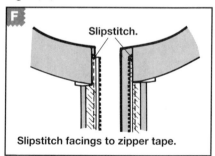

Slipstitch.

Slipstitch facings to zipper tape.

Q I always have difficulty with back slit plackets in pull-over blouses—they ravel and pull away from the stitching after several washings. What can I do to prevent this?

33

A Try this technique—a favorite in ready-to-wear:

✂ Instead of cutting the blouse back on the fold, cut it with a center back seam, placing the foldline ⅝" from the selvage (A).

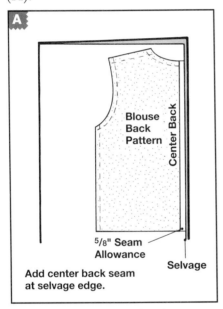

Blouse Back Pattern

Center Back

5/8" Seam Allowance

Selvage

Add center back seam at selvage edge.

✂ Stitch the center back seam up to the placket opening; backstitch.

✂ Press the seam open, pressing under the seam allowances in the placket area; topstitch

around the "placket" opening (B).

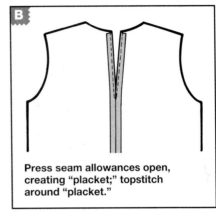

Press seam allowances open, creating "placket;" topstitch around "placket."

Q How can I accurately mark buttonhole placements on double-breasted styles?

34

A To avoid the problem of buttons not matching their buttonholes, never mark the button placement from the pattern until the buttonholes are completed. Also, be sure to mark the center front line from neckline to hem on both fronts, using a water-soluble marker or basting stitches for later reference in the button/buttonhole application process (A, page 40). This mark should remain visible on the garment until you're ready to attach the buttons. Then follow these steps:

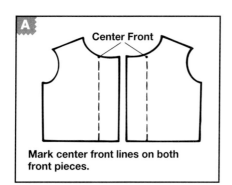

Mark center front lines on both front pieces.

✁ Make the buttonholes using the location markings on your pattern piece.

✁ Carefully lap one front over the other with center front lines matching; pin securely.

✁ Insert a straight pin into both layers through the slit in each buttonhole, placing the pin point ⅛" from the buttonhole end closest to the outer edge (B).

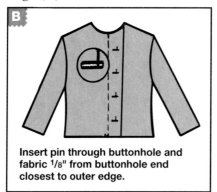

Insert pin through buttonhole and fabric ¹/₈" from buttonhole end closest to outer edge.

✁ Carefully lift the buttonhole away, leaving the pin position intact, and mark the point where the pin enters the bottom layer, using tailor's chalk, a tailor's knot or a water-soluble marker (C).

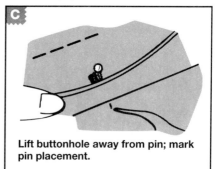

Lift buttonhole away from pin; mark pin placement.

✁ Stitch buttons in place at the marks, leaving a thread shank to accommodate the overlapping fabric thicknesses, and button the garment.

✁ Using the pattern as a guide, mark the nonfunctioning buttons' positions, making sure they line up with the functioning buttons (D).

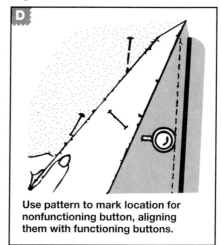

Use pattern to mark location for nonfunctioning button, aligning them with functioning buttons.

Q **How can I prevent the nonfunctioning buttons on double-breasted jackets from drooping?**

35

A The following techniques will help you solve that problem:
✂ It's easiest to simply choose flat or small-shank button styles, as larger shank loops cause the button to sit farther away from the garment, resulting in drooping.
✂ Also, try stitching shank buttons a little more tightly, but be careful not to create an obvious pucker or wrinkle under the button.
✂ Or, if you're skilled at making small eyelets, you can sink a button shank through the overlapping garment layer and use a small safety pin or cotter pin (from the hardware store) to secure it on the inside (A). This method has been used on military jackets for easy removal of gold buttons before cleaning. Some of the newer sewing machines can be programmed to make eyelets, so it's not as difficult as it might seem.

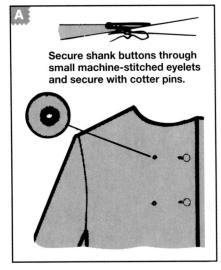

Secure shank buttons through small machine-stitched eyelets and secure with cotter pins.

Note: Some loop shank buttons are secured to the cards on which they are sold with cotter pins; if you like this idea, consider saving the pins for this purpose.

Q **I am forever replacing metal blazer buttons on jackets, even though I use double, waxed topstitching thread to stitch them. How can I prevent this?**

36

A This frustrating problem is caused by the rough edges on the metal button shank rubbing and cutting into the thread during normal wear. Try this technique to prevent it:

✂ Thread a metal looped eye from a hook and eye set through the button shank (A), then hand stitch the eye in place with doubled thread or buttonhole twist.

A

Insert looped eye fastener through button shank; sew eye in place.

Q I have some large, beautiful, antique mother of pearl buttons that have become dull. How can they be polished?

37

A Try making a smooth paste of water and bicarbonate of soda and apply it to the button surface with a *soft*-bristled brush, such as a toothbrush. Rinse the buttons thoroughly and polish them dry with a soft cloth.

Q **Does it really matter whether a man's shirt buttons left over right and vice versa for a woman's shirt?**

38

A As far as most women are concerned, it really doesn't matter a bit. But don't make the mistake of putting the buttonholes on the women's side when making a man's shirt or jacket. No one would probably ever know the difference, but *he* will! Check out unisex patterns and garments, and you'll find they always button left over right.

Q **I love buttons and use expensive ones on some items I sew. Unfortunately, I've had several sets ruined at the dry cleaners. Short of removing them every time I have the garment cleaned, is there any way to protect buttons from dry-cleaning solutions?**

39

A Better dry cleaners will often remove buttons for you—for a price, of course. These two methods are other alternatives: Try wrapping each button securely in aluminum foil or, better yet, use hook-and-loop tape, following these steps:

✂ Cut a square of hook-and-loop tape that's slightly larger than the button.

✂ Make a slit in the loop portion of the square and slip the button through it.

✂ Cover the button with the hook portion, and press the tape together securely around the button (A).

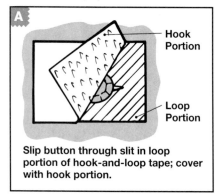

Slip button through slit in loop portion of hook-and-loop tape; cover with hook portion.

Your favorite buttons should come through the dry-cleaning process with color and finish in perfect condition.

Q 40

I want to make shirts and skirts with gripper snaps. How are they applied?

A Packaged gripper snaps—available in the notions department of most full-service fabric stores and through notions mail-order catalogs—are packaged with instructions for application. However, the following tips may also prove helpful:

✂ For best results, don't try to use any of these types of fasteners on extremely thick or spongy fabrics or through many layers. If the fabric is too thick but you still want to use gripper snaps, opt for snap tape.

Note: You can purchase snap tape or make your own by attaching gripper snaps to wide twill tape and sewing the tape to the garment using a zipper foot.

Q 41

How can I apply gemstones and nailheads to fabric and finished garments?

A Available in fabric store notions departments and through mail-order notions catalogs, gemstones and nailheads are packaged with application instructions. And no special tools are necessary, other than the eraser end of a pencil or a thimble. One additional tip to follow:

✂ To prevent the prongs from slipping out of knit fabrics, fuse a small bias square of lightweight woven fabric or interfacing where the nailhead or gemstone will be applied.

Q **How can I prevent the metal from showing through on my covered buttons?**

42

A Just follow these simple steps:

✂ Cut a circle of matching lightweight lining fabric or lightweight interfacing the same size as your fashion fabric circle.

✂ Place the lining or interfacing circle on the fashion fabric circle wrong side.

✂ Assemble the button following the manufacturer's instructions—no show through!

Q **How should I grade the layers of the front facing seam on a jacket with a collar and lapels?**

43

A This simple technique creates a perfectly rolled edge:

✄ After stitching the facing and undercollar to the jacket and upper collar, press the seams open using a contoured pressing board to get into curved and pointed areas.

✄ Clip the seam allowance at the end of the lapel roll line (A). *Note:* The lapel roll line should be marked by twill tape applied earlier.

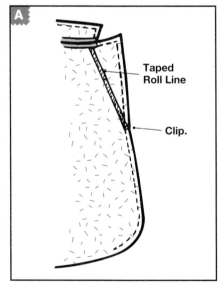

A

Taped Roll Line

Clip.

✄ Below the clip, trim the jacket seam allowance to ¼" and the facing to ⅛". Above the clip, trim the facing and upper collar seam allowances to ¼", and those of the jacket and undercollar to ⅛" (B). To remember which layer should be wider, note the wider layer in a graded seam allowance should lie next to the side of the garment that will show.

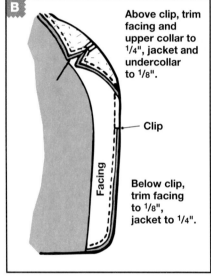

B

Above clip, trim facing and upper collar to 1/4", jacket and undercollar to 1/8".

Clip

Facing

Below clip, trim facing to 1/8", jacket to 1/4".

Note: If you've used a fusible interfacing, you can trim the layers a little narrower, because the fused interfacing stabilizes the edges and prevents raveling.

✄ After trimming, turn the garment right side out and press the finished edge: Roll the collar edge to the underside and the lapel edge toward the garment right side from the collar notch to the end of the roll line (where you made the clip and the grading changes direction). Roll the remaining front edge toward the facing (C). Steam press using a tailoring clapper to force the steam into the layers and create a smooth, flat, thin edge. Allow to dry thoroughly.

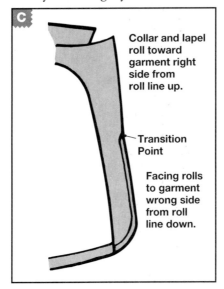

Collar and lapel roll toward garment right side from roll line up.

Transition Point

Facing rolls to garment wrong side from roll line down.

Topstitching should be a breeze when the edges have been treated this way.

Q **I'm an experienced seamstress, but I can't conquer the lapel and collar on blazers. They always curl up and won't lie flat against the shoulder and chest area. What am I doing wrong?**

A This is a common problem in tailoring. The following steps

should help rectify your dilemma:

✄ Before cutting, compare the upper collar and undercollar pieces and the jacket front and front facing pieces to be sure they allow for turn of cloth (the extra fabric needed for the upper collar and facing to roll over the undercollar and jacket lapel). With notches and dots matching, the facing should be *at least* ⅛" larger than the jacket front; the upper collar should be ⅛" larger than the undercollar.

For mediumweight fabrics, the difference between pieces should be about ¼", for heavy coatings, as much as ⅜". If your pattern doesn't comply with these standards, add to the outer edges of the upper collar and to the facing as shown (A).

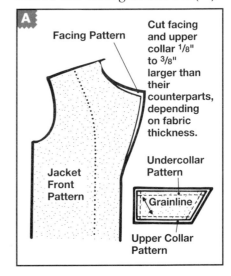

Facing Pattern

Cut facing and upper collar ⅛" to ⅜" larger than their counterparts, depending on fabric thickness.

Jacket Front Pattern

Undercollar Pattern

Grainline

Upper Collar Pattern

✂ When ready to sew the facing and upper collar to the jacket and undercollar, use a tailor's blister to control the extra fabric allowed for turn of cloth, tucking out the excess from the collar and lapel points (B).

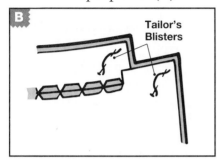

Tailor's Blisters

✂ Trim, grade and press as described in Question No. 43 (pages 45-46).

✂ For the best results, baste close to the pressed edges using silk thread or a single strand of darning cotton or embroidery floss. Leave the basting in until the jacket is completed.

If you follow these steps routinely but still have problems, the next steps may be the correction you need:

✂ Try on the jacket and adjust the collar, lapel and facing so they're flat and smooth against the shoulder and chest. Pin the facing to the jacket along the roll line and continue around the neckline (C). Ask someone else to do this when fitting your own jackets.

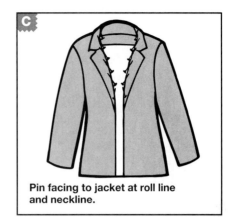

Pin facing to jacket at roll line and neckline.

✂ Remove the jacket and baste the collar and lapel to the undercollar and jacket on the pinned roll line, removing the pins as you go. Use only silk thread or a single strand of darning cotton or embroidery floss. Lightly steam the roll lines and allow to dry.

✂ On the inside, hand stitch the collar and jacket neckline seams together *as they lie* (D).

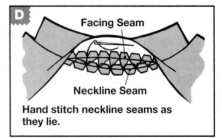

Facing Seam

Neckline Seam

Hand stitch neckline seams as they lie.

Don't worry if the seamlines don't line up. Forcing them to match can cause collar points to curl and will expose the back neckline seam. Use a long running stitch to catch the seam allowances together.

✂ Lift the front facing and using a loose catchstitch, secure it to the jacket interfacing at the roll line as pinned. Since this is a permanent stitch and must not show on the right side, catch only a thread of the facing and take a larger stitch in the interfacing.

✂ As a final check, make sure the lining fits properly. A too-tight lining can pull on the lapel and cause the points to curl outward.

Q **I'm ready to start sewing tailored jackets. How do I establish collar and lapel roll lines when the pattern doesn't include them?**

A For the most accurate placement without making a jacket test muslin, ask for the assistance of a friend, then follow these steps:

✂ Fit and permanently stitch the jacket body and permanently set in the sleeves. Apply the interfacing to the undercollar following the pattern guidesheet and stitch the center back seam. Trim the seam to ¼" and press it open.

✂ Hand baste the undercollar to the jacket neckline, carefully matching center backs, shoulders, notches and dots; backstitch securely at the notch points (indicated by dots), leaving the undercollar seam allowance free (A).

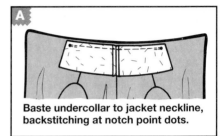

Baste undercollar to jacket neckline, backstitching at notch point dots.

✂ Try on the jacket over the types of garments you plan to wear with it. *Carefully* matching the center front lines, pin the fronts together at each buttonhole.

Standing in front of a full-length mirror, adjust the collar and lapels so they lie smoothly, and have your friend use a lead pencil to carefully mark the roll line on the right lapel and the undercollar right half.

✂ Remove the undercollar, true the roll line and transfer it to the remaining undercollar half (B).

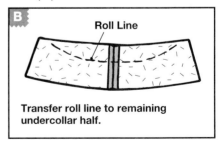

Roll Line

Transfer roll line to remaining undercollar half.

✂ Using a ruler, true the lapel roll line, ending it ¾" to 1" below the top button placement (C). Repeat the lapel roll line marking on the left lapel.

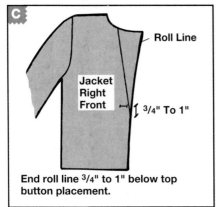

Roll Line

Jacket Right Front

¾" To 1"

End roll line ³/4" to 1" below top button placement.

✂ Tape and shape the lapels and undercollar using your favorite tailoring methods.
✂ If you plan to use the jacket pattern again, transfer the roll lines to the pattern tissue for future reference.

Q **Since I allow for turn of cloth with a tailor's blister, I don't understand why the lower lapel points on my tailored jackets always seem to curve in. Is there a way to correct this?**

46

A The solution is a simple one. When stitching the lapel and facing together, stitch the upper seam-

line in a slight outward bow to prevent the illusion of the inward dip you describe (A). Normally, this isn't necessary on the outer edge of the lapel seam.

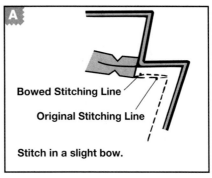

Bowed Stitching Line

Original Stitching Line

Stitch in a slight bow.

Q **Why do the notched collars on my jackets always pucker and pull? I don't have that problem with the notched collars of sewn blouses.**

47

A The difference in sewing results is likely the result of the difference in weight and thickness of the fabrics and interfacings used in blouses and jackets with notched collars.

For superior pucker-free notched collars in coats and jackets, complete the stitching in four sections:
✂ Pin the upper collar and facing unit to the undercollar and jacket.

✂ Stitch the collars together from each notch to the center back, overlapping the stitching and being sure to move the neckline seam allowances out of the way before stitching. For best results, begin and end a stitch or two shy of the dot marking the notch location (A).

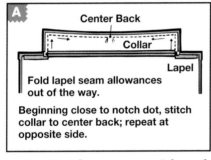

Center Back

Collar

Lapel

Fold lapel seam allowances out of the way.

Beginning close to notch dot, stitch collar to center back; repeat at opposite side.

✂ Repeat the process with each lapel in the same manner (B).

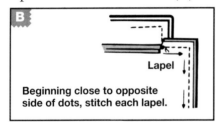

Lapel

Beginning close to opposite side of dots, stitch each lapel.

✂ Tie off all threads using a dressmaker's knot. Trim and grade all seam allowances closely to remove as much bulk as possible, and press the collar and lapel seams open over a point presser before turning right side out.

48 *Q* **What is the proper way to insert collar stays?**

A The following technique works beautifully:

✂ Determine the stay placement by folding the collar pattern at the point so the center front edge meets the lower edge of the collar. Press a crease to form the pocket stay line, then mark it on the pattern tissue (A).

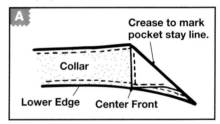

Crease to mark pocket stay line.

Collar

Lower Edge   Center Front

✂ Transfer the stay placement line marking to the wrong side of the undercollar only.

✂ From your fashion fabric, cut two collar stay pockets the shape of the front half of the collar pattern (B).

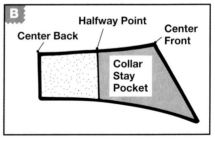

Halfway Point

Center Back   Center Front

Collar Stay Pocket

✂ Make a ½"-long buttonhole on the pocket stay line 1½" from each collar point, backing

each buttonhole area with a small piece of fusible interfacing for stability; slash the buttonholes open (C).

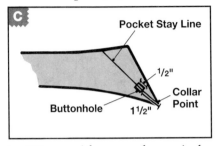

✄ Wrong sides together, stitch the collar stay pockets to the undercollar and stitch ¼" away

from the stay placement line on each side (D).

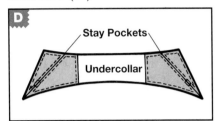

✄ Complete the collar following the pattern guidesheet. Insert the stays through the buttonholes on the undercollar; remove the stays for laundering purposes.

49

Q How can I determine if a fabric's grain is hopelessly crooked *before* I purchase it—while it's still on the bolt?

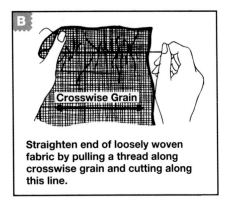

Straighten end of loosely woven fabric by pulling a thread along crosswise grain and cutting along this line.

A You're wise to recognize that off-grain fabrics can be the source of potential sewing problems; if fabric isn't "square" or grain-perfect, your finished garment won't hang properly. If you have any doubt about grain perfection before purchasing, ask the clerk to straighten the end of firmly woven fabric by tearing along the crosswise grain (A). For soft, stretchy

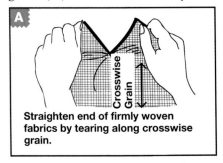

Straighten end of firmly woven fabrics by tearing along crosswise grain.

or loosely woven fabrics, the end can be straightened by pulling a thread along the crosswise grain and cutting along the line created from the pulled thread (B). Then unroll a yard or so from the bolt and fold it in half lengthwise, matching the selvages and the cut or torn end. If the cut ends must be forced to stay together and

stubborn wrinkles appear at the fold, the fabric is off-grain.

Generally, fabrics of natural fibers—silk, wool, linen and cotton—can be easily straightened by steaming (blocking) and/or stretching the fabric on the bias (C). However, if natural-fiber fabrics have been treated with a permanent-press finish, straightening the grain is usually impossible. Natural fibers blended with tough, wiry synthetics like nylon or polyester are often more adverse to straightening, too.

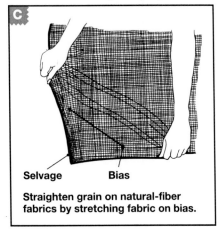

Straighten grain on natural-fiber fabrics by stretching fabric on bias.

Many 100-percent synthetic-fiber fabrics and synthetic blends are also impossible to straighten. If the degree of grain imperfection is not extreme (D), however,

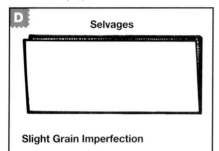

Slight Grain Imperfection

you'll probably experience few, if any, noticeable problems in sewing or flaws in the garment's final appearance. Do avoid extremely off-grain fabrics (E) and stripes, plaids and other one-way designs that are printed even slightly off-grain, as the deviation will *always* be obvious.

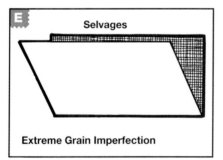

Extreme Grain Imperfection

50 Q I use lots of patterns designed for stretch knits only. Can I use these patterns on woven non-stretchy fabrics?

A This is not recommended. Because knits-only patterns vary from pattern to pattern in the degree of stretch and the type of knit required, it's difficult to give you any solid guidelines for adapting them for woven fabrics. In most cases, the time and effort required to adapt the knits-only pattern for use with wovens—coupled with the uncertain results—would deem it more sensible to buy a new pattern designed specifically for wovens.

One "safe" option, however, is cutting full, loose-fitting patterns for sweatshirt-style garments from wovens instead of the knits for which they're designed. Silky sweatshirts with ribbed-knit necklines, cuffs and hipbands convert well from knits-only status and are easy to sew and fun to wear for a slightly dressier sweatshirt look.

For other knits-only pattern types, these general hints might help:

✂ Allow *extra-wide* seam allowances in all major fitting areas.

✂ Compare flat pattern measurements at the bustline, waistline and hipline to those of standard patterns for woven fabrics to help you determine how and where to enlarge the knits-only patterns.

Q **I recently realized moth larvae had infested some feathers; I had no idea feathers were on their diet list. How can I protect my clothing/ fabrics against moth infestation?**

51

A Moths are the most well-known fabric eaters, but carpet beetles, silverfish and some types of roaches are also known to damage fabrics. Protein fibers, including wool and silk; specialty fibers, such as cashmere, camel hair and angora; and even feathers are food sources for these insects—but they will eat any fiber to get to the protein fibers. This means man-made and synthetic-fiber clothing stored on top of or next to protein-fiber garments can be damaged by insects eating their way to the main course.

Clothing stored with food stains and other soiling are especially appealing to insects and invite them to dine— regardless of the fiber content.

Insects damage fabric during the larvae stage of development when eggs laid on fabrics hatch and feed on the fibers. The common element is storage of garments—the insect eggs thrive on dark, undisturbed conditions found where you store your clothing from one season to the next, for example.

Some methods for damage control you can practice yourself include cold storage and insect-repelling odors, such as moth balls. These will not only deter insects, but will actually kill the larvae *if used properly*. To be effective, moth balls must be in air-tight storage conditions—a handful of moth balls scattered on a closet shelf will not do the job. Similarly, a cedar block placed in a closet or drawer will make your clothing smell wonderful, but will not deter insects.

The following guidelines will help control insect damage to clothing during storage:

✂ Clean garments before storage and store immediately after cleaning. Just one wearing will allow fabric to collect perspiration, food stains, etc., and hanging in a closet for a day or two is enough time for insects to lay eggs in the fabric of just-cleaned garments.

✂ Store cotton and linen items completely free from starch. Not only will starch promote the growth of molds and mildew, silverfish are especially attracted to starch as a food source.

✂ When garments are stored for long periods of time, remove and inspect them periodically for evidence of insect infestation.

✂ Store garments in air-tight conditions. This is often difficult, since storage in plastic bags isn't recommended (plastic holds in moisture which can accelerate the growth of molds and mildews). As an alternative, use boxes or larger containers that can be shut tightly.

✂ Store clothing in acid-free conditions. Materials typically used for long-term clothing storage contain acids that can weaken and discolor fabric; tissue paper, cardboard and wood are potentially harmful. For the best storage environment, line cardboard boxes with acid-free paper or use clean, white cotton fabric (muslin, old sheets, etc.) as a wrapping material and a barrier between fabric and wood or cardboard.

52 *Q* **Can you recommend a simple, sure-fire test for determining whether or not prospective yardage has anti-static properties built into it?**

A Testing for static control in fabrics is difficult because the degree of static buildup depends on a combination of three factors: the fiber content, the amount of friction to which the fabric is exposed and the moisture content in the air.

Generally, fibers with low absorbency, such as polyester and nylon, cause more problems with static buildup. Fibers with high absorbency, including cotton, linen and rayon, rarely cause static problems. Wool and silk, exceptions to this rule, have chemical components that also contribute to static buildup.

Static builds up when the fabric rubs against itself or other objects. These static charges will either be conducted away, unnoticed, or will build up on the fabric surface and cause an unpleasant shock when brought into contact with another conductor, often the human body. A cold, dry environment intensifies the problem.

Static is controlled by either treating the fiber with a finish to increase the conductivity in the fiber or by altering the fiber or yarn during manufacturing. Most finishes are temporary and are removed in the first cleaning, so fabrics that appear static-free in the store may not stay that way. Fabric softeners and anti-static sprays are consumer-applied methods for temporarily controlling static.

Q **Can you explain the little holes along the selvage of some fabrics?**

53

A Tenter holes are formed on the selvage when the fabric is clipped or pinned on a tenter frame which holds the fabric straight and taut during finishing and drying in the manufacturing process. Selvages are generally heavier than the fabric they "frame" to withstand the tension from the pins, and the holes remain as evidence of the procedure. The old expression, "I'm on tenterhooks"—meaning one is feeling a high degree of stress—originates from this textile finishing process.

Q **Is it true that the raised side of the holes along the selvage indicate a fabric's right side?**

54

A You are referring to the tenter holes (see Question No. 53). Most fabrics are finished in a "face up" position, and the raised holes would indicate the fabric right side. However, there are exceptions, so this is not a fool-proof method for determining the fabric right side.

If the fabric right side is extremely difficult to determine, though, either side would probably be acceptable for use as the right side—as long as you're consistent when assembling the garment, making sure the same side of the fabric is used as the right side of all garment pieces. If not, subtle differences between the right and wrong sides of the fabric might become apparent in the form of slight color or textural changes in the finished garment.

For easy identification, use a chalk pencil to mark an X on the wrong side of each cut fabric piece.

Q How can I judge ribbing quality? I purchased one piece because it was an excellent color match, but when I applied it and pressed the seam, the ribbing went flat. Did I do something wrong, or was the ribbing of poor quality?

55

A Generally speaking, it's unwise and unnecessary to press ribbing seams, no matter what the fiber content. It sounds like the ribbing you used was made of acrylic, which literally can't "take the heat" without losing its stretch. Polyester and nylon ribbings are much more stable. Ribbings containing a bit of Lycra® are especially nice—they're the most stable and don't stretch out of shape as readily as any of the others. Cotton/Lycra or wool/Lycra ribbings are particularly effective, and although these blends are a little more expensive, they're worth it.

If you need to crease ribbing, finger-press it firmly.

56

Q Will cutting out garment pieces on the crosswise grain, rather than the lengthwise grain, affect the finished garment?

A Yes. Differences between lengthwise and crosswise fabric grains result in performance differences on finished garments. For example, lengthwise yarns are stretched more tightly than crosswise yarns during manufacturing, meaning fabric has more shrinkage potential in this direction as yarns return to their pre-stretched size. For the same reason, if a woven fabric has any stretch or give, it's usually more prominent in the crosswise direction.

Also, fabrics typically have more yarns in the lengthwise direction, resulting in greater strength in this direction.

And novelty yarns, such as slub or loop yarns, incorporated into a fabric are most often found in the crosswise direction, because crosswise yarns are subjected to less stress and friction as the fabric moves through the loom.

The most important performance difference, however, is drape. Fabric cut on the lengthwise grain drapes more naturally than fabric cut on the crosswise grain. These differences might not be noticeable on very small garment pieces, but larger pieces will showcase the discrepancy. For example, an entire garment cut on the crosswise grain would appear fuller and less flowing than the same garment cut on the lengthwise grain.

Q **I was recently informed the term "virgin wool" doesn't indicate high quality. Is this true?**

57

A Yes, this is true. The terms used for labeling wool need some clarification for fashion-sewers to make educated choices:

The Wool Products Labeling Act regulates the labeling of wool fabric according to the amount of processing it has received, since the quality of the wool fiber is reduced with each reprocessing.

The terms "wool," "new wool" or "virgin wool" are used to identify wool that hasn't been processed. Wool bearing any of these labels has been used in the fabric for the first time. But this doesn't necessarily indicate quality. A wool fiber's quality depends upon the sheep of its origin— the sheep's breed, health and conditions under which it was raised. Therefore, a low-quality wool fabric could be truthfully labeled "virgin wool." Better indications of high-quality wool would be luxurious look and feel of the fabric and a manufacturer known for producing quality fabrics.

"Reprocessed wool" indicates wool reclaimed from previously processed wool that has never been used in a garment. For example, wool yarns or scraps of unused fabric may be shredded back to the fiber stage and reprocessed into fabric.

"Reused wool" is a fabric or other product made from previously used wool fabric. For example, old sweaters or coats may be shredded for use as oven mitt batting, coat interlining and other functional uses, but rarely to be used in fashion fabrics.

Q **58**

How does Harris Tweed differ from other tweeds?

A A tweed fabric is defined as a course woolen fabric with a somewhat wiry, hairy surface and a soft, flexible texture. The yarns frequently have small color flecks differing from the primary yarn color.

A Harris Tweed is a specific tweed fabric handwoven on the islands of the Outer Hebrides off the northern coast of Scotland. Among this chain of islands is the island of Harris, from which the fabric takes its name. The fabric is woven in the islanders' homes and marketed through the Harris Tweed Association. The orb and cross is the registered trademark of the association and identifies an authentic Harris Tweed. Although these tweeds don't differ in construction or appearance from other types of tweeds, their high quality and origin give them a timeless appeal.

Because Harris Tweeds are handwoven, keep in mind they're narrower—36" wide or less—than most mass-produced fabrics. As a result, you'll need more fabric than you would usually buy and your pattern layout will require some adjustments. Remember to use a "with nap" layout as you would with any woolen fabric.

Q **59**

How can I identify fabrics less or more prone to pilling?

A All fabrics have a tendency to form pills, which form when short fibers roll up on the fabric surface due to abrasion. And it's almost impossible to determine how much a fabric will pill without testing it. However, pilling is less noticeable on some fabrics than others, and the following guidelines will help you choose fabrics that tend to pill less:

✂ Check the fiber content. Avoid fabrics made from blends of polyester, nylon, silk or other high-strength fibers, because, if untreated, they have a fairly high tendency to pill. Instead opt for cotton, wool, rayon or blends thereof.

✂ Check the yarn twist. Highly twisted yarns will pill less than those loosely twisted. Pull a single yarn from a cut edge and try to untwist it; if it comes apart fairly easily, it is loosely twisted, and fibers should be easily worked to the surface by abrasion.

✂ Check the fabric surface. A soft, slightly fuzzy surface means more fibers protruding from the yarns and a higher potential for pilling; smooth surfaces pill less.

Q **I'm a beginning fashion-sewer and need advice on selecting the best fabric for a particular garment. Can you help?**

60

A Your fabric choice will make or break your sewing project, so you're wise to question the correlation between fabric and silhouette—time spent selecting fabric is never wasted. The first place to start is on the back of the pattern envelope where the pattern designer has listed fabric types appropriate for the pattern, as well as those inappropriate. If you find this listing somewhat limiting, consider selecting fabric on your own, but keep these guidelines in mind:

✂ Fabric construction. Does the pattern state the garment should be made of woven or knit fabric? Some styles work equally well with either type, but others are designed for specific kinds of fabric, and the pattern envelope will indicate if either is required.

✂ Fabric weight and drape. These characteristics work in tandem and are critical for carrying out a garment's design lines. A common mistake is selecting a fabric too lightweight for the garment.

Patterns with many construction details require soft, drapable fabric; if the garment has smooth, tailored lines, a firmer fabric is required.

✂ Surface design and color. The pattern envelope will state which design features to avoid, such as prominent diagonal lines or uneven plaids. A good general rule to follow dictates that the more construction details a pattern has, the simpler the fabric design should be.

Choose a fabric color compatible with your personal coloring. If possible, check the color in natural light because colors can change slightly between natural and indoor lighting.

✂ Fiber content and care. Be sure the garment style, fiber content and care requirements are compatible. For example, use easy-care (machine washable and dryable) fabrics for items you'll wear often; splurge on more delicate (dry-clean-only) fabrics for special occa-

sion garments that will be worn infrequently.

✂ Quality. Price alone is not sufficient criteria for judging fabric quality. Look for these characteristics: a flaw-free appearance; on-grain designs; high thread counts (number of yarns per square inch); if knitted, a resiliency to spring back to its original shape after being stretched; and the name of a reputable fabric manufacturer.

Q **Why are some fabrics more prone to wrinkling than others?** 61

A This depends on the fiber type, the fabric construction, the presence or lack of finishes or a combination of the three.

Fiber type is probably the most influential factor. A fiber is made of long chains of molecules held together by forces within the fiber. If these forces are strong, as in wool, they resist bending and pull the fiber back to its original shape after it has been bent or crushed. Cotton, on the other hand, wrinkles severely because molecular forces are broken when the fiber is bent and reform in the bent position, thus retaining the wrinkle.

Most synthetic fibers top the wrinkle-resistant list, and wool is the most wrinkle-resistant natural fiber. The cellulosic fibers (cotton, linen, ramie, rayon) are the most wrinkle-prone.

Fabric construction is another consideration. For example, knits resist and shed wrinkles more efficiently than wovens, because the loop structure of knits gives the fabric yarns the ability to stretch and shift in relation to bending and crushing.

However, we even see variation in wrinkle-resistance of wovens: Those with plain, smooth surfaces wrinkle more quickly than those with ribs, wales or any type of raised surface design.

Q **Is rayon a natural fiber? I thought it was man-made.** 62

A In the categories of natural and synthetic fibers, rayon lies somewhere in between. While rayon must be manufactured, the raw materials of the fiber—cotton linters, wood pulp, etc.—are natural. The fiber is chemically similar to cotton, with differences in fiber performance due to the manufacturing process.

Rayon may have a variety of different properties engineered into the fiber, depending upon the desired end use, so it's difficult to make general statements about the fiber performance. However, rayon is absorbent, comfortable and doesn't melt under heat, making it more like a natural than a synthetic.

Q **I love washed silks. What type of sewing and care is required of this fabric?** **63**

A This dress-weight fabric is washed by the manufacturer to create textural interest and easy care, requiring no pressing and allowing handwashing and line drying of even the most vivid and dark-colored varieties. Be sure to check care instructions, however, as some of these fabrics are even machine-washable and darker-colored varieties must be washed separately.

Sewing techniques for washed silks are the same as for any dress-weight silk. The two primary considerations are controlling fabric slippage during layout and stitching and concealing inner construction,

both of which tend to be slightly less troublesome due to the wrinkled nature of washed silk.

64 **Q** **I'm learning to sew with knits. What is the difference between single knits, double knits and jersey knits?**

A You refer to just a few of the knit types available today, but these terms are the most common. First, remember not to let the terminology overwhelm you. In many cases the most important criteria for selecting knit fabrics is the amount of stretch, weight and drape. The following is a brief discussion of single and double knits based on these criteria.

Single knits are similar in structure to the kinds of knits made by hand knitters.

Jersey is the most common single knit for dresses, T-shirts and underwear because it has a flat, smooth surface and excellent drape. Featuring a definite front and back, the front is identified by wales (vertical rows of loops), while the back is recognized by courses (horizontal rows of loops). This light- to mediumweight fabric

curls on the edges when stretched.

Ribbed knits are single knits used frequently for cuffs, neckbands and anywhere a high degree of stretch is desired. They look the same on the front and the back, with wales on both sides, are much heavier and bulkier than jersey knits and don't curl at the edges when stretched.

Double knits are made on machines with two sets of needles to create fabric resembling two fabrics knitted together. While these knits have two-way stretch, which varies considerably, they're usually much more stable than single knits. As a group of fabrics, double knits are generally heavier and firmer than single knits, but they range from lightweight and pliable to heavyweight with little drape. Compared to single knits, they're less likely to stretch out of shape and don't run or curl at the edges when stretched.

Interlock is another knit term you may have encountered, and it's certainly worth noting. In terms of stretch and weight, this fabric falls somewhere between single and double knits, resembling a single-knit jersey in amount of stretch, tendency to run and smooth, flat appearance; like a double knit, it's heavier and firmer than single-knit jersey, doesn't curl at the edges and is identical on both sides, resembling the face side of single jersey. Popular uses for this fabric include dresses, tops and underwear.

Q **65** **Do you know of actual ages implied when referring to "children's sleepwear" in regard to fabric flammability?**

A Children's sleepwear regulated by flammability legislation includes sizes 0 to 14 rather than ages, as children vary tremendously in clothing sizes at any given age. This size range will take children from infancy into grade school. Sleepwear and the fabrics intended for this use must be self-extinguishing or be incapable of supporting combustion once the source of the flame is removed.

Q *66* **I made yarn and fabric Christmas tree ornaments and would like to fireproof them. What is the best way to accomplish this?**

A Since all fabrics burn, it isn't possible to make them truly fireproof. "Fire-resistant" is the term used to describe fabrics that burn at a relatively slow rate and cease to burn once the flame source is removed, and this may be achieved by using yarns and fabrics that already have flame-resistant qualities.

However, since your ornaments are already completed, your alternatives are more limited. If the ornaments will withstand moisture, you may rinse them in a solution of 30-percent boric acid and 70-percent borax. This treatment will increase the flame-resistance of the ornaments, but will also reduce the softness and drapability of the fabric. *Note:* This is a temporary finish and must be reapplied if the ornaments are cleaned.

Q *67* **I plan to sew children's sleepwear and have received conflicting information on flame-resistant finishes— some say the flame-resistance on all fabrics washes away in the first few washings. Is this true?**

A No. Fabrics are either treated with chemicals to increase flame-resistancy or are manufactured using naturally flame-resistant fibers. If a fabric has been treated for flame-resistancy, the finish, according to federal standards, must remain effective for a minimum of 50 washings and dryings. And the effectiveness of naturally flame-resistant-fiber fabrics will obviously remain permanently.

However, laundry methods can affect the flammability of any fabric: Finishes can be rendered ineffective if body oils, soaps, fabric softeners, hard water deposits, etc., are allowed to build up on the fabric surface; and chlorine bleaches may destroy the finish. Therefore, follow these guidelines when cleaning flame-resistant fabrics: ✄ Wash all garments in warm water with phosphate detergents. *Note:* If these have been

banned in your area, use a heavy-duty liquid detergent.
✂ Avoid soaps and fabric softeners.
✂ Use only non-chlorine bleaches, if bleaching is necessary.

Q **Can you recommend an underlining for the bodice of a strapless dress or a bodice that just needs a little extra body?** **68**

A Silk organza (not synthetic) is a wonderful underlining for dressy fabrics that will be dry-cleaned. It's as light as a feather, adding a little body without any noticeable weight.

For washable fabrics, try cotton batiste. Swiss batiste is the lightest and finest variety and also the spendiest. Other favorites include lightweight cotton/polyester broadcloth or poplin—both are available in a wide variety of colors and suitable for many fabric types. *Note:* Be sure to preshrink the fashion fabric and the underlining you've chosen before cutting out the garment.

Q **69** **I replaced my coat lining with a new lining possessing "windbreaker" qualities only to find it's uncomfortable and cold next to my skin. Can you recommend a warmer option?**

A It sounds like you may have used a nylon or polyester lining. Both are strong and long-wearing, but notorious for creating a cold, clammy feeling—especially when worn in more humid climates. Lining fabrics made of rayon, acetate or blends of these fibers are much more absorbent since they are from natural materials. The trade-off is they're not as long-wearing as their synthetic counterparts.

When comfort is your key concern, choose the more absorbent lining with the understanding that you may need to replace it more than once if your coat gets lots of hard wear. When you do use a rayon or acetate lining fabric, take care not to overfit the lining to avoid placing wearing strain on it.

Q 70 I'm planning to sew with Ultrasuede®. What type of patterns are recommended for this luxury fabric?

A Follow these guidelines and enjoy this special fabric:

✂ Choose patterns featuring simple lines and minimal pattern pieces. Check out the "very easy" designs in the pattern catalogs, and look for patterns that offer guidesheets with special sewing techniques for synthetic suede. You'll usually find this noted on the catalog page and the pattern envelope.

✂ Choose patterns suitable for woven fabrics; knits-only patterns don't offer enough wearing ease.

✂ Look for sleeve designs with minimum ease. Kimono, raglan and other dropped-shoulder designs are easier than set-in sleeves, especially if you've never worked with Ultrasuede before.

✂ Although Ultrasuede gathers nicely, choose designs with minimum fullness. A little fullness from a yoke or minimal easing in a skirt waistline are possibilities.

✂ Waistline yokes on skirts and pants are good choices because they eliminate darts.

When choosing dart-fitted styles, look for designs with narrower darts for a smooth fit or eliminate them from the design before cutting.

✂ Avoid designs with curved seaming—it's difficult to join concave and convex curves smoothly in this fabric. Choose designs with straighter seams and use topstitching to draw attention to them.

✂ Consider using the synthetic suede as an accent or contrast with woven or knit fabrics. Collars, cuffs, yokes and band trims look great in this opulent fabric. This is the perfect approach for developing cutting and sewing confidence with this special and expensive fabric.

Q 71 Why is it so difficult to find patterns appropriate for diagonal-print fabrics?

A Many fashion-sewers share your frustration. Sometimes you have to just use your own best judgement when choosing patterns for diagonals. The following guidelines will help you make the best choice:

✂ Choose simple designs with few seamlines, since matching

these fabrics in cutting and sewing takes real planning.

✄ Avoid lots of shaped seams.

✄ Choose jacket designs with one-piece rather than two-piece sleeves.

✄ Opt for straight-cut, fitted or gathered skirts and jackets, dresses and tunics with straight lines rather than curved lines.

✄ Avoid collars and lapels in tailored garments; the diagonal design lines or weave will run in different directions on the collar points—very distracting to the eye.

✄ Simple cardigan shapes are a wise jacket choice.

✄ Choose pants and trousers with classic lines for the best results.

Q **I have a lovely border print fabric. What type of skirt pattern—other than a dirndl—would complement such a fabric?**

72

A Because border prints follow a straight line even though the design may consist of curved lines, it's difficult to use shaped pattern pieces as they cause matching problems and design distortion. A perfect skirt style for border prints features

unpressed pleats around the waistline or several deep pleats in the front and soft gathers in back (A).

Skirt patterns appropriate for border prints include those with soft, unpressed waistline pleats and those with fewer wider pleats in front and soft gathers in back.

73 *Q* **How much ease is needed in knit fabrics to achieve a good fit?**

A Because knits range from stable and nonstretchy to very stretchy, it's difficult to offer exact ease standards. For the best results and trouble-free sewing and fitting, it's wise to use patterns designed specifically for knits whenever possible. The pattern companies print a stretch gauge on the back of the pattern envelope to help you choose fabric with the appropriate amount of stretch for the design. Read the list of suggested fabrics carefully, too, and follow the pattern's recommendations.

Q 74
I want to sew swimwear on my new serger. How do I gauge pattern alterations for use with stretchy Lycra®?

A Most swimwear patterns are designed for stretchy knits and include a stretch gauge. If you purchase one of the suggested fabrics with the appropriate amount of stretch, you shouldn't need to make additional changes in the pattern, with the exception of standard pattern adjustments for a good fit.

Be aware that some swimsuit patterns are designed for two-way stretch fabrics *only*. Cut the suit so the greatest amount of stretch goes around the body for the best fit. Unlike other knits, the greatest amount of stretch is usually in the lengthwise direction. Test the stretch before laying out the pattern.

Q 75
I'm very sensitive to formaldehyde and must avoid all fabrics treated with it. Do all rayon/polyester blends and cotton/linen blends contain this chemical?

A Assume they do unless you have specific knowledge to the contrary. Since the mid-'60s, most fabrics with any cellulose fiber (cotton, linen, rayon, etc.) have received some type of finish for wrinkle-resistance and shrinkage control—usually formaldehyde because it gives good wrinkle-resistance with less damage to the fabric than some of the other options.

Because it isn't always possible to determine by look or touch if a fabric has received a finish, contact the fabric manufacturer directly to inquire about specific fabrics. Request addresses, phone numbers, fabric names and order numbers from your fabric store if this information is not listed on the bolt end.

Q Why is the word "intarsia" used to describe multi-colored sweaters?

76

A Derived from an Italian word meaning inlay, intarsia is used to describe patterns knitted into solid-colored backgrounds. These designs, frequently geometric or floral, tend to be found in a single area on a sweater rather than repeated uniformly as in the case of a jacquard knit.

Q I plan to sew a jumper from a Madras plaid. Do I need to worry about the color bleeding and running?

77

A Madras fabric—which takes its name from Madras, India, its city of origin—is defined as a fine cotton fabric, hand woven with a plaid, check or stripe pattern. The vegetable dyes used in this Indian fabric of many years ago had a tendency to run when wet, giving the fabric a soft, blurred effect—and a reputation for non-colorfastness.

However, if your Madras is from the recent crop of Madras look-alikes, it may not be Madras, but rather a Madras-look, machine-woven fabric that's completely colorfast.

To check your particular fabric for colorfastness, dip a sample in hot water; if color releases from the fabric, you're likely the owner of a true Madras. To care for your Madras garment, hand wash it separately in cold water. And remember: If some color bleeds or runs, your Madras is simply gaining a characteristic that verifies its authenticity.

Q I've noticed pima cotton is used in sheeting and other fabrics. What is pima cotton?

78

A The name Pima comes from Pima County, Ariz., where early forms of this cotton type were grown. Developed by crossing American cotton with Egyptian cotton in 1903, the resulting fiber is fine and long. It is used in household textiles, shirts and dresses. Although Sea Island cotton is generally considered the finest cotton grade, pima is also a fine grade, and the name is frequently included on a label to indicate a high-quality fiber. A word of caution, however: A high-quality fiber doesn't automatically indicate quality in other steps of construction. Be sure to check for quality in fabric construction, as well as end product (garment, sheets, etc.) construction.

Q79 **I recently made a pleated skirt of wool flannel, a fabric suggested on the pattern envelope. The skirt wrinkles when I sit in it for any length of time. Is there a remedy?**

A Unfortunately, the conditions created by long periods of sitting in any wool garment—heat and moisture from perspiration—can cause excessive wrinkling. But one of the beauties of good-quality woolens is the ability to shed wrinkles when allowed to hang overnight.

In addition, adding a lining to pleated wool skirts can help. Cut the lining as you would for a straight skirt, rather than adding the extra bulk of pleats. Make it fit comfortably and catch it in the waistline seam only.

To keep pleats sharp and crisp and make them easier to press when wear distorts them, try this trick: After the skirt is hemmed, edgestitch the inner edge of each pleat through all thicknesses, including through the hem (A). No more guessing where pleat foldlines are when it's time to press the skirt!

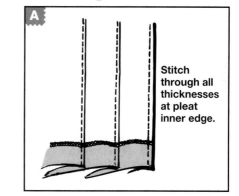

A

Stitch through all thicknesses at pleat inner edge.

Q80 **How can I fringe fabric for a shawl?**

A Before you begin, test the fabric to make sure it will fringe easily: If it's easy to remove a yarn by pulling across the grainline at the cut edge without yarn breakage, the fabric will be easy to fringe. Follow these steps for the best results:

✂ Carefully cut the fabric so the edge is on the straight of grain; mark the desired fringe depth with an air- or water-soluble marker, making sure the line follows a yarn exactly.

✂ Set the machine for a tiny zigzag stitch and stitch on the marked line to act as an anchor for the fringe (A).

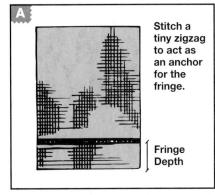

A

Stitch a tiny zigzag to act as an anchor for the fringe.

Fringe Depth

✂ Using the point of a pin and starting at the fabric edge, lift the yarns and pull away, one at a time, until you reach the stitched line (B).

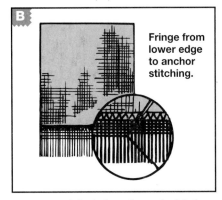

B

Fringe from lower edge to anchor stitching.

For added depth and thickness at the fringed edges, cut a strip of the same fabric 1" deeper than the fringe. Fringe this piece and stitch it behind the first fringe.

81 **Q** **Can you advise me on how to make denim fabric appear stone- or acid-washed?**

A You can duplicate the stone- or acid-washed look, using a pumice stone and bleach:
✂ Soak the denim in hot water for one hour to soften the fabric; wring out excess water.
✂ Spread the fabric flat, smoothing out all wrinkles. Rub with a pumice stone until areas of white fabric appear, avoiding rubbing too long in one spot and creating holes or near-holes. *Note:* If you can't find pumice stone, try a fine grade of sandpaper.
✂ Set your washing machine water level to low, the water temperature to hot and add ¼ to ½ cup of detergent. Add three cups of non-chlorine bleach (1½ cups of chlorine bleach for 100-percent cotton fabrics only) and allow the machine to agitate for a few minutes before placing the fabric in the washing machine. *Note:* Use less bleach if a darker fabric is desired.
✂ When the wash cycle is completed, remove the fabric and machine dry.
   Note: This process, as well as the commercial stone-washing processes, damages the fab-

ric to some degree, so experiment on a small piece of fabric before attempting larger pieces.

Q **I purchased a pattern that recommended using matelassé, a fabric that appears textured and unusual based on the photo. What is matelassé?**

A Matelassé comes from a French word meaning cushioned or padded. Although early forms of the fabric were actually padded to create a bubble effect on the surface, today's version is lightweight, thanks to a combination of special yarns and weaving techniques. Using a double-cloth construction method, regular yarns and crepe (high-twist) yarns are interlaced in patterns determined by jacquard or dobby looms. During wet finishing processes, the crepe yarns shrink, causing the bubbling effect on the fabric surface. When used for fine dress fabric, rayon or acetate fibers are often used for an elegant luster that enhances the surface's quilted effect.

True matelassé is sometimes copied in an embossed form with the raised pattern pressed in by heat. These imitations are attractive, but not nearly as durable, since the patterning may compress and flatten during wear. To determine the difference, check the thread count in the patterned areas. True matelassé should have a higher thread count where the crepe yarns have shrunk to cause puckering. Close inspection should also reveal the two types of yarn used: smooth regular yarns and bumpy crepe yarns.

Q **I have a beautiful piece of gold lamé and am anxious to sew with it. Can you give me some pointers?**

A Lamés and other metallic fabrics must be handled carefully to prevent breakage of the metallic yarns and to maintain the fabric's sheen. Following a few simple guidelines will guarantee beautiful results:

✂ Select a pattern with few design lines and an unconstructed fit. Lamés don't ease well so seek out styles that control fullness by other means, such as pleats or tucks.

73

✂ Use the "with nap" pattern layout for even shading of garment pieces.

✂ Fabrics with metallic yarns can be irritating next to the skin, so plan to line the garment or encase seam allowance edges with a sheer tricot binding. Cut facings from lining fabric or another smooth fabric.

✂ Use a fine needle and change it often to prevent damage to the fabric from dull or chipped needle surfaces.

✂ Stitch only once, as metallic yarns may be broken by repeated stitching.

✂ Use extreme caution when pressing, as metallic yarns are heat-sensitive. A cool, dry iron is best, since steam will dull the fabric and heat could melt the yarn surface. To be extra safe, try finger-pressing seam allowances or press with the blunt edge of a wooden point turner.

✂ Fuse lightweight tricot interfacing to the lamé wrong side before cutting intricate appliqué shapes. The extra body will help tame ravelly edges.

Q 84 **I'm planning to make my daughter a velvet party dress but have never sewn with velvet. Can you offer any special tips?**

A The pile surface of velvets and velveteens requires a few special considerations during layout, pressing and stitching. Attention to the following will yield the best results:

✂ Because the pile is directional, use the "with nap" layout for even shading of garment pieces. While most garments are constructed with the pile positioned in a downward direction, it's actually a matter of choice. Velvets and velveteens with the pile positioned downward have a slight silvery cast; pile in the upward direction gives a deeper, richer color.

✂ Take extra care during pressing to avoid crushing the pile: Always press on the fabric wrong side, using only as much pressure as needed; use a needle board or a scrap piece of the velvet under the fabric to help maintain the beauty of the pile surface; and set the iron temperature on low and use a press cloth if the velvet has any acetate content.

✂ Start your project with a new needle.

✂ Test stitch on a double layer of the fabric to see what adjustments may be necessary, as the pile surface may cause uneven feeding. If the seam looks puckered, try loosening the upper tension. If slippage is a big problem, try pin-basting or even thread-basting. Using a roller foot or even feed foot on your machine may further reduce the problem of uneven feeding.

✂ If skipped stitches occur, clean your machine to remove loose pile fibers that may accumulate on the machine surface.

Q **I plan to copy a beautiful satin holiday dress spotted in ready-to-wear but need some advice on sewing satin. Can you help?**

A Satin requires special care in construction and handling. These tips should help:

✂ Use a "with nap" layout for even shading and color of pattern pieces.

✂ Place pins in the seam and hem allowances, never beyond, to avoid marring the surface area of the garment.

✂ Mark on the fabric wrong side with an air-soluble marker or tailor's chalk. Test-mark on a sample.

✂ If possible, line or underline fitted bodices or skirts to reduce the wearing strain so seams don't spread and shred around the stitches. Don't overfit satin, but rather allow a little extra room in fitted garments for better wear, fewer wrinkles and a more comfortable fit.

✂ Raveling is a primary problem with this slippery fabric, so seam finishing takes top priority:

• The best finish is to overlock edges with a serger before stitching the seams.

• If serging is not an option, apply a very thin line of seam sealant to all cut edges (before handling or stitching) to stabilize them during construction.

• For lightweight satins, French seams are also a good choice. Finish the seams of heavier satins with zigzagging or binding, using a zigzag stitch to apply it.

✂ To control puckering while stitching conventionally, set the machine for 8 to 12 stitches per inch and hold the fabric taut behind and in front of the presser foot.

✂ Use the tip of the iron to open seams, pressing over a seam roll to avoid seam imprints on the right side.

Always use a press cloth and a light touch when pressing on the fabric right side. Use steam sparingly as some satins water-spot.

✄ Choose smooth-surfaced buttons to avoid unsightly snags and pulls.

Q Do you have tips for handling sequined fabric?

86

A First and foremost, choose a simple pattern with few seams and darts for the best results and simplest sewing. Look for designs with an easy fit and avoid zippers, buttonholes, pleats and gathers. Then follow these cutting, marking and sewing tips:

✄ To avoid skin irritation, line the sequined area of the garment so seam allowances are covered. Line the garment to the edge to eliminate facings and hems.

✄ Use a "with nap" layout, with the sequin edges toward the garment lower edge.

✄ Hold pattern pieces in place with masking tape and cut pieces single-layer with the fabric right side up, cutting through the masking tape (A).

The tape will control the edges of the cut sequins.

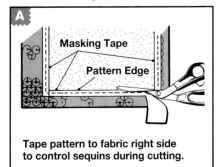

Tape pattern to fabric right side to control sequins during cutting.

✄ After cutting, use a few pins to hold the pattern pieces on the fabric pieces until you're ready to sew. Use tailor tacks or thread tracing to transfer construction marks.

✄ Use a *new* size 14 or 16 needle.

✄ To prevent sequin loss, staystitch the fabric pieces on the seamlines. Stitch on the fabric right side to prevent sequins from catching on the feed dogs.

✄ Use a pin to remove any loose sequins from the seam allowances and set them aside for later repairs, if necessary. Secure the threads by "sticking" them to the base fabric with drops of a liquid seam sealant. Allow the sealant to dry.

✄ Stitch the seams with your machine set for 8 to 10 stitches per inch. Stitching through sequins will dull the needle quickly, so replace it frequently.

✂ Because sequins are heat-sensitive, press seams open using the blunt end of a point turner or your thimble, running it along the seamlines.

✂ *Do not* use steam for the final pressing; it will destroy the sequins' sheen. Final press at a low setting and run the tip of the iron along the seamline only.

✂ Examine the completed seams and replace any broken sequins with those you set aside; hand stitch the sequins in place.

Q How can I test fabric for fiber content? I often buy unmarked remnants and would like to determine this to identify the correct care procedures.

87

A The easiest test to perform at home for fiber content is a simple burn test. Hold a small snippet of fabric in tweezers and light it with a match or lighter over the sink. Observe the color of the smoke, the ash or residue and the odor. In general, if the ash is soft and the odor is of burning hair or paper, the fabric is a natural fiber. Synthetic fibers burn with an acrid, chemical or vinegar-like odor and leave a plastic bead. If you suspect the fabric is acetate, place a scrap in a small amount of fingernail polish remover. If you're right, the fabric will dissolve.

Testing for fiber content gets complicated, of course, when dealing with blends of natural and synthetic fibers. The residue may exhibit characteristics of all the fibers involved and the odor may be difficult to define. Consult the chart (A) for a complete description of burning results for the most

A

TEXTILE BURN TEST

FIBER	BURN RESULTS
ACETATE OR TRIACETATE	FLAMES AND BURNS QUICKLY; MELTS INTO BRITTLE, BLACK BEAD; SMELLS LIKE HOT VINEGAR.
ACRYLIC	FLAMES AND BURNS RAPIDLY WITH HOT, SPUTTERING FLAME; MELTS INTO HARD, BLACK, IRREGULAR BEAD; ACRID ODOR.
COTTON OR LINEN	IGNITES ON CONTACT WITH FLAME; BURNS QUICKLY AND LEAVES AN AFTERGLOW WHEN PUT OUT; LEAVES LIGHT, FEATHERY, GRAY ASH; SMELLS LIKE BURNING PAPER.
NYLON	BURNS; MELTS INTO HARD, GRAY, ROUND BEAD; SMELLS LIKE CELERY.
POLYESTER	PULLS AWAY FROM FLAME; MELTS INTO HARD GRAY OR TAN ROUND BEAD; CHEMICAL ODOR.
RAYON	BURNS WITHOUT FLAME OR MELTING; LEAVES LIGHT, FLUFFY RESIDUE; ODOR LIKE BURNING PAPER.
SILK	CURLS AWAY FROM FLAME WITH SLIGHT MELTING; BURNS SLOWLY; LEAVES SOFT BLACK ASH; SMELLS LIKE BURNED HAIR.
SPANDEX	BURNS AND MELTS; LEAVES SOFT, STICKY RESIDUE; CHEMICAL ODOR.
WOOL	CURLS AWAY FROM FLAME; BURNS SLOWLY AND SELF-EXTINGUISHES; LEAVES BRITTLE, SMALL, BLACK BEAD; SMELLS LIKE BURNED HAIR.

common fibers. For additional information on fiber identification, consult a college textile textbook.

Q Since most fabric stores no longer give out care labels for fabrics, the information is only printed on the bolt end—and sometimes that's obscured by price tags and other labeling. Usually I can see the number that corresponds to care techniques, but what do the numbers mean?

88

A Here's the fabric care technique prescribed by the Federal Trade Commission (A).

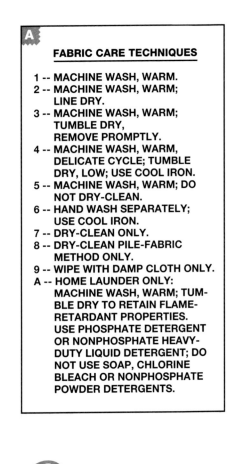

FABRIC CARE TECHNIQUES

1 -- MACHINE WASH, WARM.
2 -- MACHINE WASH, WARM; LINE DRY.
3 -- MACHINE WASH, WARM; TUMBLE DRY, REMOVE PROMPTLY.
4 -- MACHINE WASH, WARM, DELICATE CYCLE; TUMBLE DRY, LOW; USE COOL IRON.
5 -- MACHINE WASH, WARM; DO NOT DRY-CLEAN.
6 -- HAND WASH SEPARATELY; USE COOL IRON.
7 -- DRY-CLEAN ONLY.
8 -- DRY-CLEAN PILE-FABRIC METHOD ONLY.
9 -- WIPE WITH DAMP CLOTH ONLY.
A -- HOME LAUNDER ONLY: MACHINE WASH, WARM; TUMBLE DRY TO RETAIN FLAME-RETARDANT PROPERTIES. USE PHOSPHATE DETERGENT OR NONPHOSPHATE HEAVY-DUTY LIQUID DETERGENT; DO NOT USE SOAP, CHLORINE BLEACH OR NONPHOSPHATE POWDER DETERGENTS.

Q Care instructions on many of today's fabrics state non-chlorine bleach only. Can you explain why and what else I can use to remove deep-set stains?

89

A Many fabrics receive one or more finishes to enhance performance, such as flame-resistance, wrinkle-resistance, etc. Some of the chemicals used in these finishing processes retain chlorine and will ultimately cause the fabric to yellow. In addition, chlorine causes some finishes to lose their effectiveness.

While the non-chlorine bleaches help maintain clean bright whites and colors, they aren't very effective in removing deep-set stains; in some cases they even treat the stain like a color and "brighten" it.

Unfortunately, few substances work as well as chlorine bleach on heavily stained items. If a garment is stained so badly you wouldn't wear it again, consider spot-treating the stain with diluted amounts of chlorine bleach, which should remove the stain. Although yellowing will probably occur, it is often a delayed reaction, allowing you a few additional wearings. Keep in mind this treatment may damage any finishes present and eventually the fabric as well, so consider it a last-chance effort for an otherwise ruined garment. Also, remember to never use chlorine bleach on fibers such as silk, wool, spandex or acetate; the extreme damage to these fabrics will be immediate.

90

Q **I enjoy the look and feel of polished cotton, but when I machine wash and dry this fabric (as recommended on the care label), the sheen simply disappears. What is the best way to clean polished cotton and how do I reapply the finish if it washes out?**

A Polished cotton describes a group of cotton fabrics with a surface luster ranging from soft to very bright. The durability of this lustrous surface also varies—a temporary finish will dissolve with one washing; a durable finish will remain through numerous washings; and a permanent finish will remain through the life of the garment—depending upon how the finish is applied.

Polished cotton is literally polished by rollers during finishing, with more rollers creating a greater shine. Then starches or waxes are often added for extra enhancement and luster, but are usually washed out in the first few washings, so dry-cleaning is

recommended to maintain the polished surface. In some cases, resins are added which bond chemically to the fibers, creating a durable or permanent finish. To determine which substances have been added to the fabric and the durability of the finish, check the bolt end. "Permanent finish" or "permanent chintz finish" are typical statements used to indicate a polished surface that will last, even through repeated machine washing and drying.

Since the polished luster is produced by rollers in the manufacturing process, it isn't possible for the consumer to recapture the surface treatment.

Q 91 **How should fabrics labeled "dry-clean only" be handled before cutting to ensure safe cleaning without shrinking?**

A For best results, follow this general rule: Pretreat the fabric using the same method you will use to clean the finished garment. If you have time or money constraints, however, you *could* steam press the entire piece of fabric on the wrong side or use the London

shrink method. This involves spreading the fabric on a damp sheet or other large piece of fabric, rolling the two layers of fabric together and allowing the garment fabric to uniformly dampen from the sheet; after an hour or two, unroll the fabric and allow it to dry flat.

Disadvantages of the London shrink method include the large amount of space necessary and the fact that some fabrics are damaged or altered by the moisture. Acetate satins and raw silks are examples of fabrics that should not be subjected to this method. Many silks are hand-washable, but test a scrap first, since dark colors can run.

Keep in mind high-quality fabric is well worth the extra time and cost of careful pretreatment; try to avoid cutting corners at this step.

Q 92 **What is the best way to wash silk fabric? Can I use a fabric softener in the wash water?**

A Launder washable silks in lukewarm water with a mild detergent or an inexpensive liquid dishwashing detergent. Shampoo can also be used in a pinch, but

it's quite expensive and contains conditioners silk fabrics don't need. If necessary, use heavy-duty detergent sparingly on heavily soiled inner neckbands and cuffs *only*—the builders in these could harm the silk if used consistently. Add a little fabric softener to the wash water, if desired, to control static electricity. It won't damage the silk.

Q I just finished sewing two rayon challis dresses, and I'm disappointed with the results. On both dresses, the hem flares at the side seams. Why did this happen and how can I correct it?

93

A It's difficult to determine the cause of your hem problem without actually examining the dresses; however, it may be the result of stitching in the wrong direction. Even with careful handling, rayon challis easily stretches out of shape, especially along cut edges that have any degree of bias. Therefore, it's critical to use directional stitching, always stitching seams from the widest to the narrowest garment area (A).

To correct the flare on your finished garments: Remove the hem and, beginning at the lower edge, stitch a slightly deeper seam for several inches, gradually tapering back to the original seamline (B). Be careful not to stretch the fabric when you replace the hem, especially if it's machine stitched.

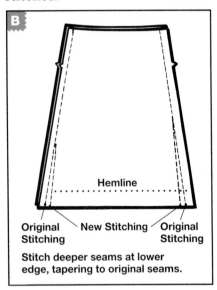

B

Hemline

Original Stitching   New Stitching   Original Stitching

Stitch deeper seams at lower edge, tapering to original seams.

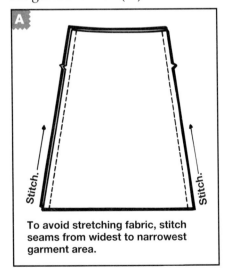

A

Stitch.   Stitch.

To avoid stretching fabric, stitch seams from widest to narrowest garment area.

Q I'm having difficulty sewing on a cotton knit fabric. The first time I stitched the hem, I used a ball point needle and stretched it while sewing (as instructed), but the results were awful—the fabric stretched out of shape. Can you suggest a remedy?

A The reason for stretching while you sew is to put the same amount of stretch in the seams as there is in the fabric. This prevents the seams from popping when you move in the garment, putting stress on the seams. Unlike seams, hems aren't normally subjected to wearing stress, so stretching isn't always necessary. It sounds like you may have stretched the hem too much while stitching. To avoid the problem in the future, do some test stitching on fabric scraps with varying amounts of stretch.

You might also try using a narrow zigzag stitch on knits. It has more "give" than a straight stitch so the knit doesn't have to be stretched as much while stitching. Another nice hem finish on knits is double needle topstitching (A). The two needles share a common bobbin thread which "zigzags"

94

between the needles on the underside.

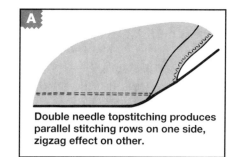

Double needle topstitching produces parallel stitching rows on one side, zigzag effect on other.

95

Q When sewing pants, I'd like to shorten them before cutting them out from fabric. What is the best way to do this?

A You're wise to recognize the advantages of shortening the pattern before sewing. To do this:
✂ Determine the desired finished length by measuring from your waistline, over the hip, to the desired length, or measure the side seam of a pair of pants that's the correct length.
✂ If your pattern has no lengthen/shorten lines below the knee, draw a line perpendicular to the grainline at a point above the hemline and below the knee, then fold to shorten the necessary amount.
✂ Blend the cutting and stitching lines at the side seams and inseams (A, page 87).

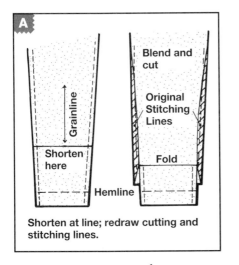

Shorten at line; redraw cutting and stitching lines.

✂ Construct as usual.

Q When shortening tapered pants, the circumference at the ankle changes and some-times causes the hem to pucker. How can I avoid these pant-hemming problems?

96

A Simply follow these steps:

✂ Measure the pant leg lower edge to determine the finished width.

✂ Cut away the excess pant leg for the desired length, leaving 1" extra for the new hem allowance.

✂ Turn the pants wrong side out and use tailor's chalk or a marking pen to draw tapering

lines on the legs: Beginning just below the knee, mark to the hemline, removing equal amounts from the side seam and inseam so the width at the new hemline is the same as on the original pant leg.

✂ To avoid a puckered hem, broaden the leg from the hem-line to the lower edge, rejoining the original stitching lines (A).

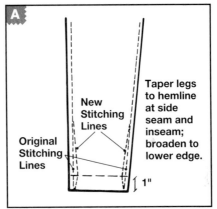

✂ Hand or machine baste on the marked lines and try on the pants to check the adjustment.

✂ Permanently stitch the new seams, remove the old stitch-ing, trim the seam as necessary and press. Press the hem under.

✂ If the hem upper edge is too full, causing bulkiness, ease-stitch the hem upper edge to gather excess fullness. If the hem upper edge is too narrow, causing puckers, let out the seams from the hemline to the hem allowance edge or taper the pant leg a bit just above the hemline.

Q I prefer the hems in my slacks to extend over the heels of my shoes in back and just touch the instep in front, but I've never been able to do this satisfactorily. Can you suggest a way to do this?

97

A What you describe is sometimes called a "cantilevered" hem and is definitely more attractive and flattering, giving the illusion of a longer leg. It takes a little preplanning to accomplish this neatly:

✂ Before you cut the pants, determine the desired pant length. Wearing the heel height you'll wear with the finished pants, measure the inseam of a pair of pants that's a comfortable length in front.

✂ To that finished length, add 2" for the hem allowance; for the extra length in back, add an additional ½" to 1" at the leg center back, tapering back to nothing at the side seams (A).

✂ Construct the pants up to the point of hemming.

✂ Clean-finish the hem edges.

✂ Easestitch the back hem allowance ½" from the raw edge (B).

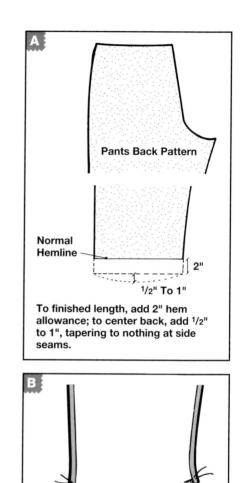

A

Pants Back Pattern

Normal Hemline

2"

½" To 1"

To finished length, add 2" hem allowance; to center back, add ½" to 1", tapering to nothing at side seams.

B

½"

Easestitch back hemline.

✂ Turn up an even-width hem allowance all around; draw up the ease to fit the back leg as needed, being careful not to draw it up too tightly. Tie off the easestitching to secure the ease, open out the hem allowance and steam the back leg area to remove as much ease as possible (C, page 89).

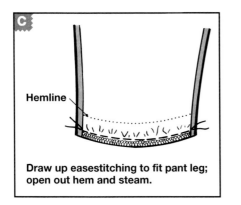

Hemline

Draw up easestitching to fit pant leg; open out hem and steam.

✂ Hem the slacks.

Q Whenever I make a circular or flared skirt, the hem doesn't hang evenly, sometimes varying as much as 3" between the center front and back and the side seams. What can I do to correct this?

98

A The problem you describe is common with bias-cut skirts. Since the seams are not cut on the straight grain, stretching can occur while handling and fitting. In fact, even after carefully marking and stitching a hem in a bias-cut garment, you'll notice the hemline doesn't always remain even. It's a fact of life that completed bias garments stretch while on the hanger, during wear and while being pressed. To control some

of this stretch, follow these handling tips:

✂ Press the skirt pieces, first pressing from the hem edge to the waistline. This will remove quite a bit of stretch.

✂ Staystitch before you sew the pieces together, especially on loosely woven fabrics, stitching ½" from the seam edges and stitching from the wide end to the narrow end on each piece (A).

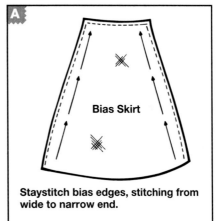

Bias Skirt

Staystitch bias edges, stitching from wide to narrow end.

✂ Assemble the skirt front and back following the pattern guidesheet, then attach the front and back to a skirt hanger and allow it to dry 24 hours so the bias give can hang out (B, page 90).

During this process the skirt may become visibly skinnier and longer. *Note:* It's important to do this step before completing the skirt for a good fit, otherwise it might become "skinnier" as you wear it.

B

Skirt Front

Skirt Back

Allow skirt front and back to hang on a skirt hanger for 24 hours.

✂ Complete the side seams (altering if needed for size changes), being sure to stitch the seams from the wider end to the narrower end, ensuring a little give by stretching the seam slightly as you sew.

✂ Press the seams flat as stitched and in the same direction as the stitching; let cool, then press the seams open. Attach the waistband.

✂ Try on the completed skirt and have someone mark the hem for you with a hem marker. *Note:* After wearing, you may still find variations in the length all the way around—sometimes as much as 3" or more—and you may need to re-hem if deviations are too conspicuous.

✂ Store extreme bias-cut garments folded in a drawer to avoid additional stretch while on a hanger. This will help retain the fit and an even hemline for a longer period of time.

Q **Do you know a method for achieving good-looking shirttail hems on the serger? I'm never satisfied with the results on a conventional machine.**

99

A Serged shirttail hems are the smoothest, neatest finish on this tricky edge. The shape of the curve at the shirt lower edge will determine which of these two methods to use:

✂ For gently curved shirttails, serge the side seams first, then serge the hem, trimming away ⅜" of the ⅝" hem allowance. Turn up the hem along the serging and topstitch (A).

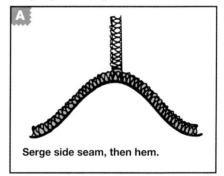

A

Serge side seam, then hem.

✂ For more sharply curved hems, serge the hem on the front

and back pieces in the same manner as above, turn up the hem along the serging and topstitch; serge the side seams (B).

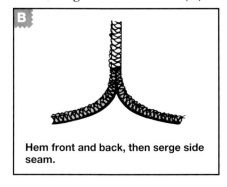

Hem front and back, then serge side seam.

of fabric should make the lower edge behave.

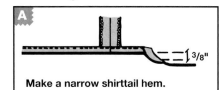

Make a narrow shirttail hem.

100

Q The hems on my striped T-shirt-weight knits always roll to the right side. What can I do to prevent this?

A T-shirt knits have a natural tendency to roll to the right side, and usually the weight of the hem will control this problem. If not, try fusing a narrow strip of lightweight fusible interfacing to the hem allowance before blindstitching the hem in place.

Or, try stitching a narrow shirttail hem: Turn under and press a ⅜"-wide hem allowance, then turn up another ⅜" and machine stitch in place (A). The extra weight of a double layer

101

Q How should hemline chain be attached to tailored jackets?

A To attach chain to the hem of a completed jacket, hold the lining hem pleat out of the way and hand tack the chain to the upper hem edge on the jacket from front facing to front facing, alternately catching the top and bottom of the links. Tuck the chain ends under the facing (A).

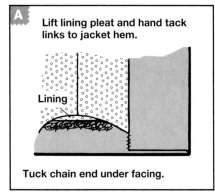

Lift lining pleat and hand tack links to jacket hem.

Lining

Tuck chain end under facing.

Q **I have a linen table-cloth stamped with an embroidery design, and I'd like to use the linen for something else. Can I remove the design?** `102`

A Since linen can be washed and is not adversely affected by chlorine bleach, try washing and bleaching the piece in your washing machine. This might remove the ink design, depending on its permanency.

First, zigzag, serge or apply seam sealant to the fabric raw edges to prevent excess raveling, then machine wash and bleach; dry to the just-damp stage and press. If this ploy only fades the stamping, consider using the stamped side as the wrong side of the fabric when cutting out your project.

Q **I want to make cloth napkins for daily and special occasion use. What fabrics are best for this purpose?** `103`

A For the most absorbent, stain-releasing napkins, use almost any fabric made of firmly woven cotton, linen or a blend of the two.

Polyester/cotton blends are another option (for maximum absorbency, synthetic fibers should be no more than 50 percent of the blend). Because polyester tends to be permanently stained by oil, however, choose a blend with a higher cotton content and pretreat with a stain repellent such as Scotchgard® (this will arm your napkins with a better chance for a long life). Or use an untreated blend and simply accept the fact that, eventually, the napkins may need to be discarded because of permanent stains.

Napkin-making offers you a perfect opportunity for being a bit creative with fabric selection. Some great bargain possibilities: Check your stash; look to the remnant bins; and shop garage sales. Also, consider using flat sheets—from your own linen closet or department store white sales. A twin variety will yield a whopping 24 16½"-square napkins.

Q I plan to make draperies and bedspreads from bed sheets. Does sheeting fabric have a lengthwise and crosswise grain?

A All woven fabrics have a lengthwise and crosswise grain, and sheeting is no exception. If you purchase flat sheets, the lengthwise grain runs from hem to hem. Lengthwise threads are stronger and more numerous to take the strain of pulling and tugging on the sheets. While it might not make much difference which way the grain runs in a bedspread, draperies should definitely be made with the lengthwise yarns running vertically as they will hang better and wear longer. When using printed sheets, it's also important to consider the direction of the print—some have a definite up-and-down patterning rather than an allover design, and one-way layouts may be necessary.

Be sure to check that the sheet print is parallel to the grainlines or your draperies may not be "visually comfortable" in your room setting.

105

104

Q I'm planning to make a fabric shower curtain and would like to add shine to the fabric I choose. Is this possible?

A Instead of adding shine, simply choose an already-shiny decorator chintz or vinyl-coated fabric for the outer shower curtain. Then hang the decorative curtain over a plain, plastic shower curtain liner for protection. The outer curtain will naturally repel accidental water splashes, but not a drenching. When making a fabric curtain, first purchase the liner, then make buttonholes in the fabric curtain to match the spacing in the liner; insert each ring through both curtains (A).

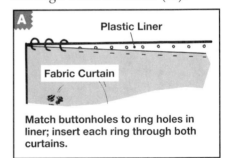

A

Plastic Liner

Fabric Curtain

Match buttonholes to ring holes in liner; insert each ring through both curtains.

Q I made some beautiful balloon shades but am unhappy with the fraying on the pull cords. Can you suggest a professional finish?

A Seam sealant to the rescue! Trim the frayed cord as neatly as possible, then coat the cut edges with a seam sealant and allow it to dry. If the pull cords are nylon, you can also opt to sear the ends using a kitchen match. When hot, the nylon fibers melt together and harden, eliminating fraying.

106

Q I want to make slipcovers for my sofa's box-style cushions. Can you suggest a technique for applying the zipper that will prevent the seam allowances from raveling in the wash?

A The usual ½" seam allowance for slipcovers may prove skimpy in the zipper area, so allow a ¾"-wide or wider seam allowance, then clean-finish the edges; when the seam allowance is turned back it will be caught by the zipper stitching.

107

108

Q I'm sewing oven mitts and pot holders for gifts. Is it true that cotton batting provides better insulation than polyester varieties?

A Absolutely not. Polyester batting actually provides superior insulating qualities, and polyester fibers manufactured specifically for batting provide outstanding loft and insulation. Plus, polyester battings are very accessible and are available in a variety of weights. Cotton, by comparison, has very low resiliency and packs down quickly, reducing the batting's insulating qualities.

109

Q I'm recovering dining room chair seat cushions with beautiful silk brocade. What type of nails should I use to prevent the fabric from snagging and pulling?

A Although no special nails or tacks are necessary to achieve the best results, the following technique for applying fabric "tacking" strips will alleviate the problem of fabric snags or runs. For each cushion:

✂ From your decorator fabric, cut the appropriate-size square for the seat cushion.

✂ From muslin or another firmly woven fabric, cut four 4"-wide strips 2" longer than one edge of the decorator fabric square.

✂ Right sides together, center and pin one strip to each edge of the decorator fabric square.

✂ Using a sharp needle, machine stitch the strips in place (A).

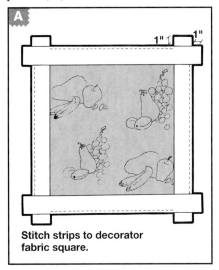

Stitch strips to decorator fabric square.

✂ Center the fabric right side up on the chair seat cushion. Pull the muslin tacking strips tautly to the cushion wrong side, inserting staples or tacks through each strip, instead of the decorator fabric, to secure it.

Q **Our home is designed so the playroom/basement windows look out onto the gravel drainage edging placed around the house. Because the windows are small, I need to take advantage of the little natural light they allow, but I desperately want to conceal the view (or lack thereof). Because of the flooding possibilities, we must keep this area free of outdoor plantings. Do you have any suggestions?**

110

A Consider doing some indoor landscaping instead. If you don't have window sills, add a shelf at or slightly below the sill line (or the height of your baskets/pots). Pick up some inexpensive French bread baskets, leaving them natural or spraying them a color to complement your room scheme, and fill with some low-light greenery, such as trailing ivy, and, if your energy and temperatures permit, a few flowering plants as well. This indoor scape will look great from inside as well as outside.

For additional indoor interest, top the window with a small tailored cornice or delicate pouf, covering just a hint of the window (A). Or, install

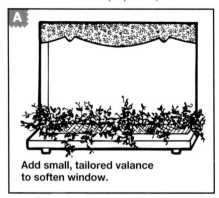

Add small, tailored valance to soften window.

two cafe rods—one at the window upper edge, the other at the lower edge—then staple or stitch some pretty ribbons at various distances between the rods to add the feeling of a trellis backdrop for your garden sill while still allowing plenty of light (B).

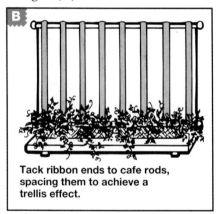

Tack ribbon ends to cafe rods, spacing them to achieve a trellis effect.

111

Q **The simple knife-edge pillows I make end up with distorted corners. What am I doing wrong?**

A When making square or rectangular knife-edge pillows, it's a good idea to slightly round the corners to prevent those unattractive points:

✂ Fold the pillow top piece in half, then in half again; mark ½" in from the corner *without* folds (A).

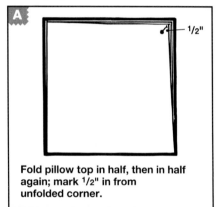

Fold pillow top in half, then in half again; mark 1/2" in from unfolded corner.

✂ From the marked corner, mark halfway to each adjacent corner, then beginning at the ½" marking, draw a line that tapers to each side edge marking (B, page 98).

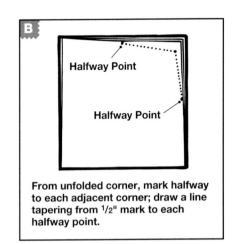

Halfway Point

Halfway Point

From unfolded corner, mark halfway to each adjacent corner; draw a line tapering from 1/2" mark to each halfway point.

✂ Cut along these lines through all layers, rounding slightly at the ½" marking, then use this piece as the pillow bottom pattern and continue with the pillow construction as usual. *Note:* Retain an even seam allowance all around and trim corner seam allowances diagonally to about ⅛".

Q **Help! I mistakenly used fusible web for interfacing in a silk blouse and didn't discover my mistake until I stitched and pressed. I've removed the stitching, but how do I remove the web without damaging the silk?**

112

A The only solvent for fusible web is rubbing alcohol—which may or may not damage the silk. And since you have nothing to lose at this point, it's worth a try.

You'll need to wash the silk to remove the alcohol, so if you didn't preshrink the silk first, be aware that some shrinkage could occur in laundering. Use warm water and a mild detergent, rinse the silk thoroughly, blot out as much water as possible and press it dry.

Q **What type of interfacing should I use for men's shirts to yield a crisp look even after washing?**

113

A Look for special non-woven fusible interfacings made specifically for tailored shirt collars, cuffs and front bands at your fabric store. When applied following

the manufacturer's instructions, they withstand laundering beautifully.

For success with any fusible interfacing, be sure to preshrink the fashion fabric and always do a test sample to see the hand and appearance yielded from the combination of your fabric and interfacing. Then, launder your test sample as you will launder the finished garment and check to see if the selected interfacing produces the results you want.

Q **I've always preshrunk my fabric. Do I need to pre-shrink notions and interfacings, too, and if so, how should I do it?**

114

A Preshrinking zippers and twill tape was once very important because of their fiber content. Now that they're made of nylon or polyester, however, the shrinkage factor is almost nonexistent. In deciding whether to preshrink trims, check the fiber content, and preshrink anything that's 100-percent cotton or linen. The easiest way to preshrink yardage of twill tape and lace is to leave it on the cardboard inner packaging or wrap it around a similar piece of cardboard if it was purchased by the yard. Bend the cardboard in half and place it in a 2-cup measure of *hot* tap water (A). Remove it after the water has cooled and allow it to dry.

Bend cardboard in half and submerge trim in hot water.

Interfacings, both sew-in and fusible, require pretreatment. Wash and dry woven sew-in interfacings to remove sizing and allow for residual shrinkage. Nonwoven sew-ins do *not* require preshrinking.

Preshrink woven, knit and weft-insertion fusible interfacings by immersing them in a sinkful of hot tap water. Allow the water to cool, then carefully squeeze the water out of the interfacing and roll in a towel to remove excess moisture; hang over a clothesline or shower curtain rod to drip dry.

To preshrink fusible nonwovens, cut the pieces following the pattern instructions. Then press the garment pieces to

which they will be fused to warm the fabric, position the interfacing "sticky" side down and steam gently with the iron held just above the fusible. If you watch closely, you'll see the interfacing pieces draw up (shrink) a little. After steaming, fuse in place following the manufacturer's instructions.

Note: Many fusible interfacings are labeled preshrunk. For best results, however, preshrink with one of the above methods anyway.

Q **I'm returning to sewing after many years and am confused by the array of interfacings now available. Can you offer some guidelines for selecting appropriate types?**

115

A It's now possible to find the perfect interfacing for any project, thanks to advances in textile technology. Keep in mind the purpose of interfacing is to support and stabilize the garment fabric without overwhelming it, therefore fabric weight, type and area to be interfaced are all important considerations. Use the following points as a ready reference when making choices:

✂ Construction. Interfacings are available in woven, nonwoven and knit varieties. A good rule of thumb is to match the type of interfacing construction with the garment fabric construction, noting that nonwoven interfacings are available in weights compatible with either woven or knit fabrics; woven and knit interfacings have superior drape; and knit and nonwoven interfacings require no edge finishing.

✂ Weight. All interfacing companies offer weights ranging from featherweight to heavier tailoring weights. Keep in mind different weights may be required within the same garment, depending upon the amount of support desired. For example, a man's shirt may need heavyweight interfacing in the collar, mediumweight in the cuffs and lightweight backing the pocket. And when selecting an interfacing weight, be sure it isn't so heavy that it's noticeable through the fabric, also keeping in mind many interfacings, especially nonwoven types, lose some degree of stiffness with wear and cleaning.

✂ Application. With today's vast selection of interfacings, a common concern is whether to use a fusible or a sew-in variety. Fusibles offer speed of application and a lot of stabilizing power. They also, however, add a degree of stiffness to most fabrics, are slightly visible and aren't suitable for napped-surface fabrics or those with any raised design feature, since the fusing application may flatten the fabric surface. Sew-in interfacing may be used with any fabric type, but the application process will be more time-consuming.

✂ Care. Be sure the care requirements for the interfacing are compatible with those for the fabric.

✂ Testing. Experiment with different types of interfacing on various fabrics to determine the most compatible combinations, labeling and saving your samples for later reference.

✂ Planning. To be prepared for any interfacing need, consider keeping an ample supply of several interfacing types in your stash.

Q **I plan to make embellished sweatshirts. What should I use to fuse fabric or Ultrasuede® appliqués to sweatshirt fleece?**

116

A Appliqués are fun and easy with fusibles. For the best results, choose a fusible web backed with a transfer paper that allows you to adhere one side of the web to fabric before cutting the appliqué from it (A). Because it's applied before cutting, the web extends exactly to the appliqué edges so there's no chance of the web getting on your iron's soleplate.

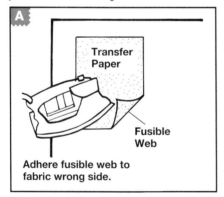

A

Transfer
Paper

Fusible
Web

Adhere fusible web to
fabric wrong side.

After removing the transfer web's backing paper from the appliqué, simply fuse the appliqué in place using a press cloth and following the manufacturer's instructions. If desired, machine edgestitch or satin stitch fused appliqués for added interest—and stability.

Another handy notion for applying appliqués is fusible thread, which contains a fusing element that bonds when heated and subjected to pressure. Use this special thread in the lower looper of your serger or the bobbin of your conventional sewing machine when doing decorative stitching around simple appliqué shapes. Then position the appliqué on the garment and fuse it in place. The thread strand remains, but the fusible element melts to hold the appliqué temporarily until you stitch it in place.

Q **I want to gather the lower edge of blouses with elastic thread in the bobbin, but have had little success. Any suggestions?**

117

A First, purchase a high-quality elastic thread with a thick rubber core wrapped in 100-percent cotton, if possible. Your local sewing machine dealer might carry it. If you're unable to find this, don't settle for less than 60-percent cotton content in the wrapping thread— nylon-covered elastic thread often loses its stretchability.

Then follow these tips:

✂ Wind the elastic thread onto the bobbin *slowly, without* allowing it to stretch.

Or, better yet, wind the elastic thread onto the bobbin *by hand* rather than by machine.

✂ Thread the bobbin case the same way you thread it with conventional thread, making sure to pull plenty of bobbin thread out of the hole in the throat plate and leaving a long tail at the end of the stitching (so you don't lose it!).

✂ Tie elastic thread ends in a square knot to secure.

✂ For elastic shirring, make several evenly spaced rows of stitching, stitching over a strip of paper while holding the fabric taut for each row and beginning and ending the stitching at a seam. *Note:* It's a good idea to experiment with stitch length on a fabric scrap—the longer the stitch length the greater the shirring effect you'll achieve.

Q **Why does the outer layer of thread occasionally bunch up above the needle as I sew? Is is poor-quality thread or does it just get old?**

118

A Thread shredding can result from a number of factors. Although poorer-quality threads may shred more easily than others (it's best to invest in thread with a reputable brand name), even the best-quality thread has an occasional weak spot.

Shredding also happens when the machine needle is too fine for the thread or the fabric you're using. A rough spot on the needle eye, throat plate or even the bobbin case could also be the culprit.

To stave off thread shredding:

✂ Discard damaged needles. If you regularly stitch over pins, your needle could be rough, especially if it has barely nicked a pin while stitching.

✂ Smooth any rough spots on the machine's throat plate using a small piece of crocus cloth, available at hardware stores.

✂ Don't use old thread, especially if it's made of a natural fiber like silk or cotton. As you suspected, some threads do weaken with age. And, if a thread shreds repeatedly, seams sewn with it may also prove weak. In general, it's better to discard old thread, rather than take a chance on ruining a garment.

119 *Q* **I thought sewing thread was color-fast, but when I pressed over some contrasting basting thread, the color transferred to the garment fabric. How can I avoid this?**

A Most home-sewing threads are indeed colorfast. Colorfast, however, is a relative term because color loss can result in a number of situations. Thread used for sewing must be colorfast to hot and cold water washing and dry heat and must resist crocking (the color rubbing off on other surfaces). Dark-colored threads, especially navy and red, tend to be the most troublesome in terms of color transfer.

To test colorfastness before using the thread:

✂ Place a length of thread on a light-colored fabric scrap and press with a dry iron; check the fabric for color transfer.

✂ Steam press the thread sample. If no color transfers, the thread should be safe to use, even for basting in a contrasting color.

120 *Q* **What is the best thread choice for sewing silk chiffon?**

A Choose either a soft, cotton thread, which will stitch smoothly and won't cut the fabric, or a very fine polyester thread designed for stitching lingerie fabrics. Avoid silk thread on sheers, as it's very strong and could cut the fabric. Also avoid cutting the seam by using a longer stitch, a super-fine European size 65 or 70 needle and testing before stitching the garment.

121 *Q* **I plan to quilt a vest and was told a platinum needle is best for quilting. Is this true?**

A Hand quilters rave about platinum-plated needles because they slide through the fabric layers effortlessly. You'll love them for any type of functional or decorative hand sewing.

However, they're quite expensive, so you'll want to keep this special needle in a safe place.

Q **"Clear" elastic is wonderfully light and easy to use and *very stretchy*. As a result of this stretchiness, however, using the measuring instructions for regular elastic results in a too-loose fit. How can I solve this problem?**

122

A The first few times clear elastic is stretched, it will elongate up to 10-percent of its original length. So, before measuring and cutting, stretch the elastic a few times, then release it. After this "warm-up" stretch, it will have 100-percent recovery.

Q **My water-soluble marker markings don't always disappear, even though I avoid pressing over the markings before trying to dissolve them. How can I avoid this?**

123

A Every notion has its advantages and disadvantages, and nothing is foolproof. Water-soluble markers work great on most fabrics, but it's important to do a test sample to determine their effectiveness before using them on your fashion fabric.

The marks on the fabric right side are the most critical. If testing shows the ink won't disappear with a drop of water, substitute tailor's chalk or one of the new powdered chalks in a plastic applicator.

Marks on the fabric wrong side that don't show through to the right side don't require removal, particularly in washable garments.

Fiber content might affect the marker results, but the fabric surface will more likely cause problems. Sizing and other chemicals used in fabric finishing processes may interact with the ink, and preshrinking by washing or dry-cleaning might solve this problem.

Q I was really excited about saving time with my new rotary cutter and mat until I realized it "scoots" the edges of new patterns and throws off the cutting line, even if I pin carefully. Short of cutting off the pattern edges, which defeats the purpose, I've yet to find a solution. Any suggestions?

A Your dilemma is understandable, but unfortunately, cutting away the pattern edges *is* the answer. In fact, leaving pattern margins on—even when cutting with shears—isn't a good idea. Cutting away the margins before pinning and cutting ensures the most accuracy.

Note: Trim the pattern margin right after purchasing the pattern—while watching the evening news, watching the kids play or simply relaxing—so the pattern is ready when you're ready to cut, which might be minutes, hours or even days later. This will help you feel that the task isn't wasting valuable time.

Q I recently purchased a mid- to lower-priced rotary cutter, which won't cut through fabric. Do rotary cutters work only on certain fabrics, or did I make the mistake of purchasing not only an inexpensive, but a cheap, rotary cutter?

A Any sharp rotary cutter should easily cut through six layers of most fabrics—if you're cutting on a firm surface (purchase a mat made specifically for rotary cutting) and the cutter is properly adjusted.

If the nut securing the blade is too tight, the blade won't glide easily through the fabric and may not cut at all. So, first loosen the nut. Also remember, it's much easier—and safer—to cut by pushing the wheel away from you, rather than dragging it toward you.

And look for bits of lint that catch between the nut and the blade after continued use, restricting cutting. Periodically remove the nut and clean and lightly oil the blade for the best cutting results.

If you feel the blade is dull, try cleaning and oiling it before discarding it. Many professional quilters (often frequent users of rotary cutters) contend you

can use a rotary cutter blade for several months of consistent cutting if you follow a regular cleaning and oiling routine.

Q **How can I laminate or somehow protect a favorite pattern so it won't become dog-eared after many uses?** 126

A A simple solution to this problem is applying a lightweight, non-woven, fusible interfacing to favorite patterns. Here's how:
✂ Cut a rectangle of interfacing slightly larger than each pattern piece.
✂ Fuse each pattern piece to its corresponding interfacing piece, using a warm iron and being careful to keep the iron from touching the interfacing margins (fuse to within 1" of the pattern edges). Allow to cool.
✂ Trim away the excess interfacing, then complete the fusing around the pattern piece outer edges.

Note: If fused patterns won't fit into their original pattern envelopes, roll them, plus the pattern envelope and guidesheet, and place them into a cardboard tube—empty paper towel tubes, for example. Then write the pattern number on the tube and store it on a shelf or in an expandable wire rack.

127 **Q** **Can you suggest a method for storing my growing collection of scissors and shears to protect them, yet keep them handy at my sewing table?**

A Look for sewing organizers in the kitchen! For example, a lazy-Susan-type kitchen utensil will store scissors and shears, as well as rulers and other sewing gadgets safely and conveniently right at the sewing machine. Also, consider hanging your scissors and shears from a mug rack hung right next to your sewing station.

Q How should I store the variety of fabrics I've accumulated in my fabric stash? Is folding preferable, or should I roll the fabrics on discarded bolts from the fabric store?

128

A Wrapping yardage on individual bolts is a good idea, but if your stash is substantial, this might take up too much room. If you can only wrap a portion of your stash, choose fabrics that crease or crush easily, wrapping them around bolts, or better yet, on individual tubes. If they must be folded, refold them periodically to avoid permanently set creases. Store the tubes in a tall wicker basket in a corner of your sewing room to add a colorful "decorator" touch.

If you have open shelving, consider storing folded fabrics or bolts in color groupings or store them by fabric type. Storing this way has some hidden advantages—you'll always know exactly what you have on hand, and seeing it every day may help curb your fabric-shopping appetite and inspire you to sew more.

129

Q I finally have a small room to call my own for sewing and wonder if you have any hints for setting up a cutting and pressing area. I don't have a lot of space or money to spend on expensive cabinets or furniture. What do you suggest?

A A sturdy kitchen cart on wheels makes a wonderful cut-and-press center for the sewing room (A).

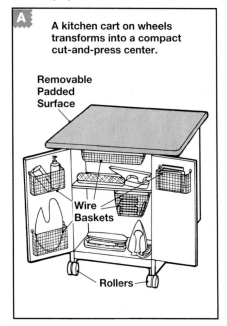

A kitchen cart on wheels transforms into a compact cut-and-press center.

Removable Padded Surface

Wire Baskets

Rollers

Make sure it's a comfortable height so you won't have to bend over it to cut—about 33" to 34" high is fairly standard. Look for one that has lots of storage space beneath. Many

have shelf-mounted pull-out wire baskets, as well as door-mounted baskets where you can store press cloths, pressing pads, marking equipment and current patterns. Tie a ribbon through the handles of your scissors and one through the hole in a ruler, then hang them from the potholder hooks on the side of the cart to keep them handy.

For a cutting surface to lay on top of the cart, pad a large piece of pressed board, ply-wood or a hollow door with wool or a natural-fiber carpet pad, then cover it tightly with heavy muslin or lightweight canvas and staple it to the sur-face underside. A 30" width will accommodate 60"-wide fabric folded in half; a 48" length will allow for the length of a coat, pant leg or floor-length skirt pattern.

This arrangement can be a real space-saver. When the cart isn't in use, simply remove the board and place it against a wall or under a bed and push the cart toward a wall. When you're ready to cut, pull it away from the wall and posi-tion the board so you can walk all around it for easy cutting.

Q I'm having trouble working with accordion-pleated fabric; it spreads out when I attempt to cut or sew it. At best, I have wavy seams and practically no pleats. Can you recommend a solution?

130

A Fabrics with small accordion pleats may double or even triple their length if the pleats aren't stabilized before the fabric is handled. To add the desired stability, use clear packing tape without reinforcement strips and the following method:

✂ Temporarily lay out the pattern pieces on a single fabric layer.

✂ Adhere 1½"- to 2"-wide clear packing tape to the fabric under each pattern piece so the tape spans both the cutting line and seamline along all pattern edges.

✂ Cut the pattern pieces from the fabric, then remove the tape from the fabric side that will *not* be next to the presser foot during stitching.

✂ Before stitching each seam, place a strip of lightweight twill tape under the seamline (next to the feed dogs) to stabilize the seam during wear.

✂ Stitch each seam through all four layers (twill tape, the two pleated fabric layers and the packing tape). *Note:* Stitching through this tape will make your needle a bit sticky, so change it often.

✂ Remove the packing tape; the tape will be perforated by the stitching and should easily tear away from the fabric. *Note:* Be sure to pull the tape sideways from the stitching line rather than in an upward direction. If you have difficulty tearing the tape away from the seam, remove the thread from the needle, and stitch over the seamline again; this will perforate the tape a second time, making it easier to tear.

If you use this method, be sure you never touch your iron to the tape. When pressing accordion-pleated garments during construction, press only in the seam allowances; pressing in the pleated areas can permanently flatten the fabric.

Q I love pleated gar-
ments, but hate re-
pressing each pleat
after a garment is washed
or dry-cleaned. How can I
permanently set pleats like
those in ready-to-wear?

A Because pleats in natural-fiber fabrics are difficult to set and usually
require re-pressing (woolens
are the exception—especially
those with a hard finish, like
gabardine), begin by choosing
synthetics or natural fibers
blended with thermoplastic
synthetics like polyester or
nylon, for your pleated garments.

To make the fabric "remember" its pleats, press each pleat
in place, and while the fabric is
still warm, replace the iron
with a tailor's clapper and continue pressing while the fabric
cools. Thermoplastic synthetics
will only "remember" the new
shape of a pleat when cool, and
a combination of the cool hard

wood and pressure will help set
the crease. Also, use strips of
paper between each pleat and
the fabric beneath to avoid
making unwanted permanent
imprints on the pleat (A).

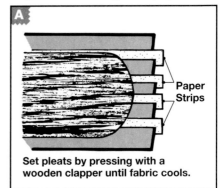

Paper
Strips

Set pleats by pressing with a
wooden clapper until fabric cools.

Note: Your pleats may never
be as "permanent" as those you
find in ready-to-wear because
manufacturers perform this
process with industrial equipment unavailable to the consumer. But using the above
method should improve your
pleating results and make main-
taining the "press" easier with
less touch-up required.

Q **I made a dress with many pleats, front and back, and the process of marking all those foldlines took forever. Can you recommend a speedier method?**

132

A If you marked the foldlines with tailor tacks or a tracing wheel, your frustration is understandable. Using a combination of snip-marking and pin-marking is a quicker, more accurate technique for marking pleats—and tucks as well. It's easiest to do on a padded or cardboard cutting board:

✂ Fold the fabric right sides together for cutting.

✂ After cutting each piece, but *before you ever move* the piece from the cutting board, snip-mark the pleat lines at the upper and lower pattern edges, just nipping into the cut edge ⅛" (A).

✂ Push a straight pin into the mid-point of every line, plus at two or four more points along the line, especially on longer pieces; remove all the pins holding the pattern to the garment edges (B).

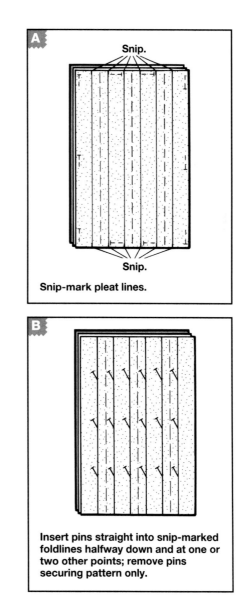

A

Snip.

Snip.

Snip-mark pleat lines.

B

Insert pins straight into snip-marked foldlines halfway down and at one or two other points; remove pins securing pattern only.

✂ Working from the cut edge to the foldline and without disturbing the pins, carefully lift the tissue away from the upper fabric layer and, using a water- or air-soluble marker (test first) or an easily removable chalk, mark the location on the first

row of pins (C). Then fold back both the tissue and fabric upper layer away from the cutting surface and mark the pin locations on the fabric lower layer in the same manner. Remove the pins from the line just marked.

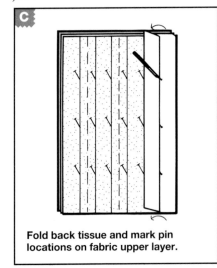

Fold back tissue and mark pin locations on fabric upper layer.

✂ Continue folding back the tissue and fabric layers to the remaining pin locations in the same manner.
✂ Immediately fold and press or fold and stitch the pleats, using the snips at the upper and lower edges and the pin markings as your guides (D).

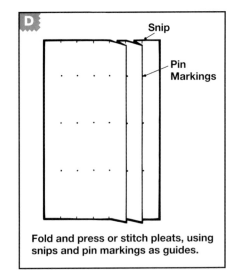

Fold and press or stitch pleats, using snips and pin markings as guides.

133

Q **I received a beautiful machine-knit suit with an accordion-pleated skirt as a gift, and it requires shortening. What is the best method for a professional look?**

A You have three options, the easiest of which is to take it to a professional dressmaker. If you'd rather do it yourself:

You might be able to shorten it from the upper edge, depending on the cut. To use this method:
✂ Cut away the excess skirt from the upper edge, saving the waistband or waistband casing section (A, page 115).

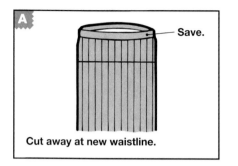

Save.

Cut away at new waistline.

✂ Machine baste the pleats flat across the upper edge, drawing up the basting to fit the skirt waistband, if necessary.

✂ Re-apply the original waistband.

If the skirt is wider at the lower edge than the waistline, which is likely the case, the easiest way to shorten it is to trim the excess length and finish the raw edge with a dense, wide overlock stitch using thread that matches *exactly*.

If you can find a very fine wool fingering yarn that perfectly matches the skirt, try threading it through the upper looper of your serger. Be sure to adjust the tension for a smooth, even stitch and practice on the discarded skirt section first.

Q 134 **What is the best way to press serged seams?**

A You'll get great results pressing serged seams following these tips:

✂ Like any other type of seam, it's important to set the stitches first by simply pressing the seam flat as it was stitched; let cool.

✂ Press the seam to one side from the garment inside.

✂ On the right side, press along the seamline, pressing toward the seam edge.

✂ If you plan to serge across a serged seam, press the first seam in the direction you plan to serge the second seam, helping you avoid twisting seams in the garment (A).

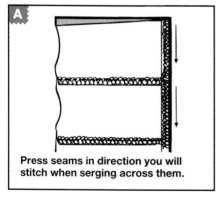

Press seams in direction you will stitch when serging across them.

Q 135 **Even though I'm careful when pressing darts so they don't imprint to the garment right side, they're still obvious in some fabrics. What can I do to correct this problem?**

A Darts are obvious because of the bulk of two layers pressed in one direction, creating three layers of fabric in one spot. To remedy the problem:

✂ Cut a 1"- to 1½"-wide bias strip of self-fabric slightly longer than the dart.

✂ Center the strip under the dart so it will be caught in the stitching (A).

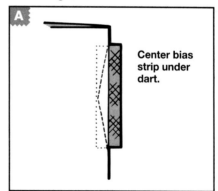

Center bias strip under dart.

✂ Press the dart in one direction and the strip in the other direction so similar layers of fabric are on both sides of the stitching line (B, page 118); trim the bias strip edges to simulate the dart shape.

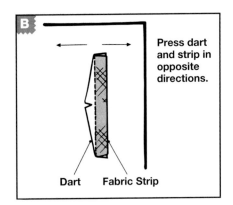

Press dart and strip in opposite directions.

Dart   Fabric Strip

Q How can I put a permanent crease into polyester suiting fabric?

136

A You may never be able to crease polyester to your satisfaction. One of the reasons polyester is so widely used as an apparel fabric is because it resists wrinkles and maintains a smooth appearance. And since a crease is nothing more than a big wrinkle, the fiber will work to smooth it out. Creases in ready-to-wear are formed by heat-setting the polyester, a process which presses the crease area almost to the melting point—460 degrees to 554 degrees Fahrenheit, depending on the type or variant of the fiber. It would be risky for you to try this at home due to the danger of permanently damag-

ing the fabric. For the best at-home results when pressing stubborn polyester, use your best pressing equipment (a good steam iron and a wooden pounding block).

137

Q What is the proper pressing technique for men's white shirts and women's blouses? Should the sleeves be creased or not?

A For men's shirts and women's tailored shirts and blouses, press the sleeves first, then follow with the cuffs, collar and front and back:

✂ Fold the sleeve in half along the underarm seam and press the upper edge, forming a crease (A).

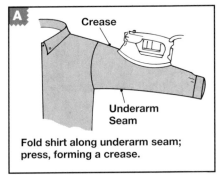

Crease

Underarm Seam

Fold shirt along underarm seam; press, forming a crease.

✂ Use a sleeve board to press the cuffs to avoid a crease (B, page 119).

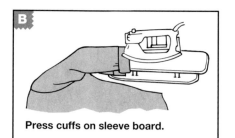

Press cuffs on sleeve board.

✂ Press the collar.

✂ Press the fronts and back—leaving them until last ensures they won't be wrinkled from pressing the other details.

For full-sleeved blouses, slip the sleeve over a sleeve board and press the sleeve and cuff to avoid a crease.

For styles with back yokes, fold the garment wrong sides together along the yoke seamline and press the yoke (C).

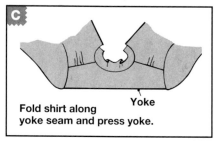

Yoke

Fold shirt along yoke seam and press yoke.

Q **I've noticed a plastic-like bead in the creases of my husband's ready-to-wear trousers, helping to maintain a perfect crease. Can I duplicate this?**

138

A To permanently set the creases in slacks you sew for yourself or your husband, use fusible thread:

✂ Locate the crease by placing the pant leg on the pressing surface, with inseams and outseams directly on top of each other, then press your crease in place, using an up-and-down motion to avoid stretching and a press cloth to prevent shine; allow to cool.

✂ Cut a strand of fusible thread a few inches longer than your crease.

✂ Carefully place the fusible thread strand within the crease fold on the fabric wrong side; press in place following the manufacturer's instructions to adhere the thread and achieve a perfect permanent crease with no telltale signs of intervention.

Or, use a tailor's clapper and pounding block along with your iron:

✂ Locate the crease as explained above.

✂ Press the crease with a steam iron and a press cloth to prevent shine, using an up-and-down motion to avoid stretching the fabric and pressing a small section at a time. After pressing each section, replace the iron with the clapper/pounding block and apply pressure (A), allowing the cool wood to absorb the heat and help the fabric "remember" the crease.

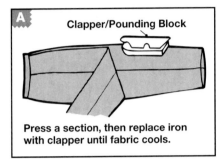

Clapper/Pounding Block

Press a section, then replace iron with clapper until fabric cools.

Q I always press as I sew, but it seems I'm replacing my steam iron every 18 months or so. One didn't put out enough steam, another developed a hot spot on the soleplate and they all seem to take a long time to start to steam once they're in the ironing position. I always put the iron on its heel while rearranging what I'm pressing. Is that the problem?

A A quality household iron should give you constant, even steaming, even if it has been on its heel between strokes. However, like every other product, iron quality varies and price is often an indicator of the quality you can expect.

In the case of your problem irons, keep in mind most irons come with a warranty. If your current iron isn't performing properly, don't throw it away until you've checked the warranty—you may have some recourse due from the manufacturer. In addition, however, you may want to consider stepping up to a more professional iron.

It sounds like you're a fashion-sewer who sews and presses a lot, which makes you a perfect candidate for a more "industrial strength" iron with added steaming power. These irons are substantially heavier than most household irons you may have used—a major plus in construction pressing and fusing. They're also more expensive. Check your local sewing machine dealers and department stores for these iron options.

Q **Occasionally, when I set sleeves into jackets and coats, I end up with front or back wrinkles. What am I doing wrong?**

140

A The wrinkles you describe are probably due to the way you've eased the sleeve into the armhole. If your shoulder shape deviates even slightly from pattern standards, you must adjust the easing to accommodate your shape. Some people need more sleeve fullness in back, others need more in front. To properly ease a sleeve in place:

✂ Carefully mark the shoulder dot, front and back notches and dots between the shoulder and notches on the sleeve pattern *and* the garment armhole.

✂ Easestitch the sleeve cap as directed in the pattern guidesheet and draw it up to fit the armhole.

✂ Pin the sleeve into the armhole, carefully matching notches and dots and paying particular attention to the quarter-point dots between the shoulder dot and the notches. *Note:* Accurate matching here ensures even distribution of the sleeve.

Also, be aware of the slight amount of ease in the underarm of a set-in sleeve; it can be con-

trolled with a few extra pins. Never shift this ease toward the sleeve cap, as the notches must match.

✂ Machine or hand baste the sleeve into the armhole on the stitching line as accurately as if you were stitching permanently.

✂ Try on the garment and examine the hang of the sleeve.

✂ If diagonal wrinkles appear in the front, release the basting from notch to notch over the shoulder and redistribute the ease, rotating the sleeve cap toward the back. If diagonal wrinkles appear in the back, repeat, but rotate the sleeve cap toward the front (A).

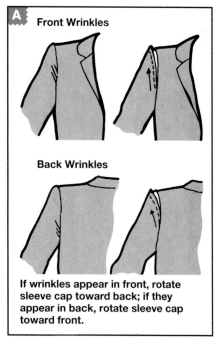

A **Front Wrinkles**

Back Wrinkles

If wrinkles appear in front, rotate sleeve cap toward back; if they appear in back, rotate sleeve cap toward front.

Note: This may cause the shoulder dot to no longer match the shoulder seam.
✂ Baste again, then check the fit. When satisfied with the hang of the sleeve, permanently stitch to secure.

Q When a pattern envelope indicates that a dress or blouse pattern has a "turn-back sleeve" or "rolled up sleeve—wrong side will show," can I improve the appearance of this type of sleeve by adding a facing and cuff?

A It's not necessary to add a facing to this type of sleeve. Rather, add a deep hem allowance that will accommodate the amount you'll turn back (A). Since you'll be turning back a double rather than a single layer of fabric when you roll the sleeve, interfacing is not necessary.

141

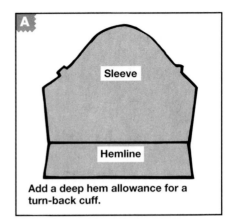

Sleeve

Hemline

Add a deep hem allowance for a turn-back cuff.

If you'd like to make the "cuff" permanent, try on and adjust the turn-back and pin it in place. Then stitch in the ditch of the underarm seam through all layers to secure it (B).

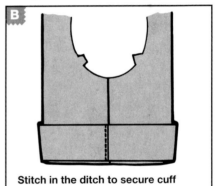

Stitch in the ditch to secure cuff permanently.

Q Sometimes my set-in sleeves wrinkle and pull at the shoulders, bind in the front armhole and feel tight across the upper back. What can I do to correct these problems?

142

A The problems you describe probably stem from the cut of the armhole and the thrust of your back and shoulders. These aren't uncommon problems, especially with more and more women spending time working at desks.

If the front armhole binds and wrinkles form across the upper back to the shoulder, your shoulder probably thrusts farther forward than the pattern allows. A shoulder seam that follows a straight line from your neck, but then twists or curves toward the back at the armhole, also indicates forward shoulder thrust (A). This figure

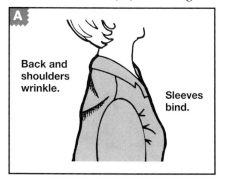

A

Back and shoulders wrinkle.

Sleeves bind.

variation is more noticeable in jackets, blouses or dresses with collars.

To correct this problem, add to the back shoulder seam at the armhole, tapering to nothing at the neck, and decrease the front shoulder the same amount (B). The amount will vary from individual to individual, so start with at least a ¼" change on your next blouse, then increase, if necessary, in successive garments.

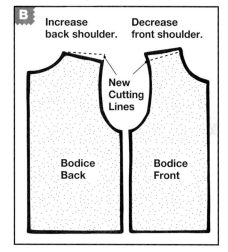

B

Increase back shoulder.

Decrease front shoulder.

New Cutting Lines

Bodice Back

Bodice Front

You may also need to rotate the sleeve forward in the armhole so the large dot matches the new shoulder seam. Baste the sleeve into the armhole and adjust if necessary.

You'll be amazed at what a difference this simple change will make in the fit and feel of your blouses and jackets.

Q **I love to wear jackets with the sleeves pushed up to the forearms—but they won't stay up! Any suggestions for making sleeves that can be worn down or pushed up?**

A A piece of elastic hidden inside the sleeve should do the trick. Try this technique in the jackets you sew or add it to readymades:

✂ Measure around your forearm just below the elbow crease (A); cut a length of ¼"-wide elastic this length, plus seam allowances.

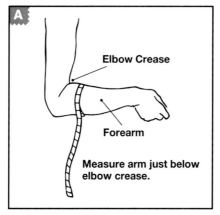

Elbow Crease

Forearm

Measure arm just below elbow crease.

✂ In an unlined jacket: After sewing the jacket sleeve seam, stitch the elastic ends to the seam allowance about halfway between the elbow and the wrist (B).

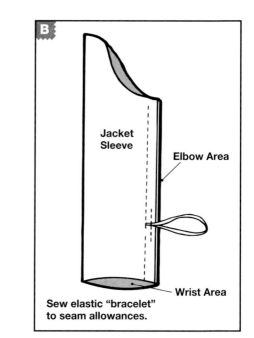

B

Jacket Sleeve

Elbow Area

Wrist Area

Sew elastic "bracelet" to seam allowances.

In a lined jacket: Catch the elastic in the lining seam allowance while sewing the sleeve lining seam (C).

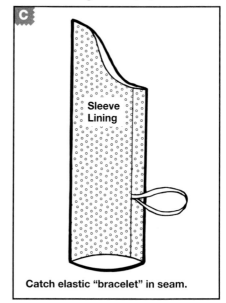

C

Sleeve Lining

Catch elastic "bracelet" in seam.

✂ When you put your jacket on, slip an arm through the elastic "bracelet" inside each sleeve; when you push the sleeves up, they should stay put.

In less-tailored jackets, as well as blouses and dresses, stitch a piece of ¼"-wide, *clear* elastic (see Question No. 122 on page 106 for a clear elastic hint), cut the same or slightly shorter than the distance around the sleeve lower edge, to the sleeve hem allowance before turning it up and hemming (D). The elastic acts as a stay to help keep the sleeve up and to prevent the lower edge from stretching out of shape from being pushed up on the forearm.

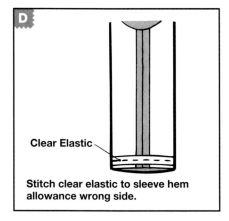

Clear Elastic

Stitch clear elastic to sleeve hem allowance wrong side.

144

Q **How can I achieve a smoother, more professional look when applying cuffs? The bulk from the seam allowances makes the placket opening edges lumpy.**

A It's much simpler—and less bulky—to attach the cuff *before* finishing the cuff ends, as most guidesheets illustrate. Here's how to do it:

✂ If possible, cut the cuff with the long, unnotched edge on the selvage, or finish the edge with serging (A).

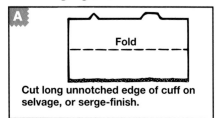

A

Fold

Cut long unnotched edge of cuff on selvage, or serge-finish.

✂ Interface the cuff and prepare the sleeve lower edge and the sleeve placket according to the pattern guidesheet.

✂ Right sides together, pin the cuff to the sleeve, matching the notches and adjusting the gathers so the cuff end seam allowances extend beyond the sleeve edges (B, page 126). Stitch and trim the seam allowances to ¼". Press the cuff/sleeve seam flat, with the seam allowances toward the cuff.

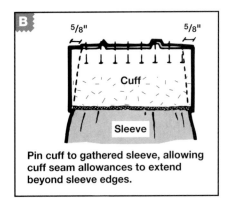

Pin cuff to gathered sleeve, allowing cuff seam allowances to extend beyond sleeve edges.

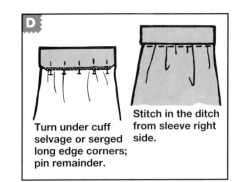

Turn under cuff selvage or serged long edge corners; pin remainder.

Stitch in the ditch from sleeve right side.

✂ Right sides together, fold the cuff on the foldline and stitch each short end slightly less than ⅝" from the raw edges to avoid catching the sleeve placket (C). Trim the seam allowances and clip the corners; turn and press.

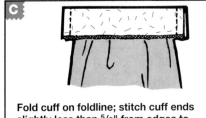

Fold cuff on foldline; stitch cuff ends slightly less than ⅝" from edges to avoid catching placket.

✂ On the serged or selvage cuff long edge, turn under each corner at an angle and pin the remaining long edge in place; to secure, stitch in the ditch of the cuff seam from the sleeve right side (D).

Note: Use the same technique when applying waistbands—it works like a charm to eliminate unnecessary bulk!

Q 145 **What causes sleeves to bind when I raise my arms? Is it the armhole or the sleeve width?**

A You've already hit on the two possible answers. If the armhole is too low, raising your arm could cause discomfort. Usually this isn't the reason, though, unless you're using the wrong pattern size.

In blouses and dresses, you should have at least 2" to 2½" of ease at the fullest part of the upper arm. In jackets and coats, the required ease increases to 3" and 4", respectively. If you don't have enough ease for a comfortable fit, adjust the sleeve pattern:

✂ Draw a line from the sleeve cap center to the sleeve hem, parallel to the lengthwise grainline. Draw a second line from underarm to underarm, perpendicular to the first line (A).

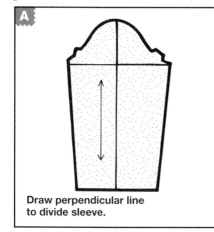

Draw perpendicular line to divide sleeve.

✂ Slash the pattern on these lines almost to the edge. Spread the sleeve until the center opening width equals the amount of additional ease needed; tape the pattern pieces together. If it was necessary to spread the sleeve more than 1", add backing paper or pattern tracing cloth and redraw the original sleeve cap (B).

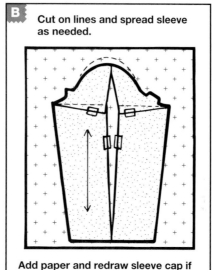

B Cut on lines and spread sleeve as needed.

Add paper and redraw sleeve cap if spread more than 1".

146

Q What is the correct way to permanently attach shoulder pads in a garment?

A Try these simple techniques:

For set-in sleeves:

✂ Try on the garment, then slip each shoulder pad into position so the edge extends ⅜" to ½" into the sleeve cap, unless the pattern guidesheet indicates otherwise. *Note:* If the shoulder pad extends too far into the sleeve, it will create a "dent" in the upper sleeve below the edge of the shoulder pad. When satisfied with the location, secure with a few straight pins on one side of the shoulder seam (A).

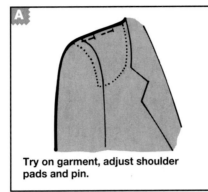

Try on garment, adjust shoulder pads and pin.

✂ Sew the pad to the shoulder seam allowance with loose catchstitching, being careful *not* to stitch through all layers of the pad (B).

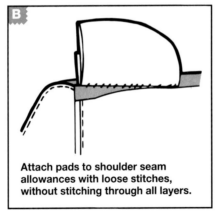

Attach pads to shoulder seam allowances with loose stitches, without stitching through all layers.

✂ Using loose stitches to allow ease between the pad and the garment, tack the ends of the shoulder pads to the armhole seam allowance at front and back (C).

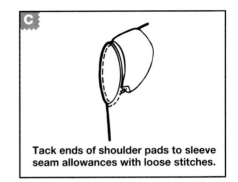

Tack ends of shoulder pads to sleeve seam allowances with loose stitches.

For dropped shoulder and raglan sleeves:
✂ Using specially shaped raglan shoulder pads, position each pad while wearing the garment. Adjust so the sleeve hangs straight from the shoulder (D).

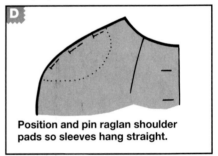

Position and pin raglan shoulder pads so sleeves hang straight.

✂ Catchstitch the pad to the shoulder seam allowance only, as described above.

Note: In tailored garments, it may be possible to loosely tack the pad to the interfacing; other garment styles may allow tacking the pad to seams or darts in the front or back shoulder area.

Q **I love the look of elasticized waist-bands with several rows of stitching through them. My dilemma: The stitching seems to remove most of the stretch. How can I correct this problem?**

147

A Unfortunately, the only way to remedy the problem in completed garments is to remove the elastic and start over. Then follow these steps:

✂ Use a nylon mesh elastic, which can withstand topstitching without losing its stretch recovery. It also doesn't wrinkle and roll.

✂ Cut the mesh elastic for a comfortable waist measurement, plus 1", and insert it through the waistline casing. Adjust the elastic to fit and stitch the overlapped ends securely (A).

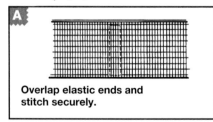

Overlap elastic ends and stitch securely.

✂ Distribute the fullness evenly, then topstitch through all layers, stretching the elastic so the fabric is taut while you sew (B).

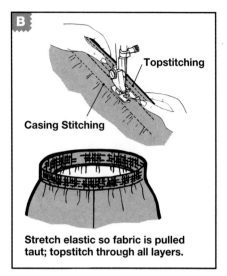

Stretch elastic so fabric is pulled taut; topstitch through all layers.

You can create the same shirred waistline look without stitching through the elastic by topstitching the casing area to create tunnels for ¼"-wide elastic. Space the rows ⅜" apart so the elastic will pull easily through the tunnels (C).

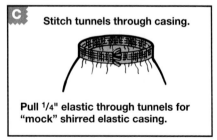

Stitch tunnels through casing.

Pull 1/4" elastic through tunnels for "mock" shirred elastic casing.

Q How can I add a knitted waistband to a simple silk blouson? Will the same technique apply for a wool or cotton single-knit jersey?

148

A You can add a knitted waistband to any fabric, knit or woven—just be sure to choose a ribbing with plenty of resiliency and a fiber content that can take the same care as the fashion fabric. Test the ribbing for resiliency by stretching; if it doesn't return quickly to its original size, choose another ribbing. Ribbings with a percentage of spandex are more resilient and long-wearing.

✄ When adding a ribbing waistband to a blouson style, the most important consideration is determining where you want the ribbing to sit on your body:

• Pin a length of ribbing around your body at that location so it fits snugly without stretching.

• Remove the ribbing carefully, leaving pins to mark the necessary length, and add 1¼" for seam allowances.

• Cut the ribbing this length and twice the desired finished width, plus seam allowances.

✄ Cut the blouson and assemble it, following the pattern guidesheet, but leave open one side seam (or the center back seam, if applicable).

✄ Mark the center of the ribbing and fold it in half lengthwise, wrong sides together; right sides together, pin it to the blouson lower edge at the open seam, matching the ribbing center to the finished side seam (or center front).

✄ Stitch or serge the ribbing to the blouson lower edge, stretching the ribbing to fit (A).

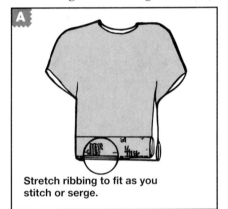

Stretch ribbing to fit as you stitch or serge.

✄ If you stitched rather than serged, straight stitch or narrowly zigzag close to the first stitching and trim the seam close to the second stitching.

✄ Complete the underarm seam, beginning at the ribbing lower edge (B, page 131).

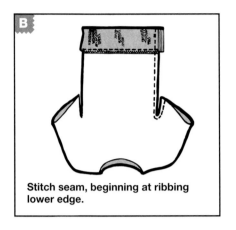

Stitch seam, beginning at ribbing lower edge.

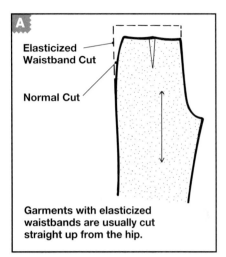

Elasticized Waistband Cut

Normal Cut

Garments with elasticized waistbands are usually cut straight up from the hip.

Q My elastic waistbands always look lumpy. What am I doing wrong?

149

A One reason elastic waistbands can be lumpy is an undesirable teaming of garment design and fabric choice. Most patterns for this waistband type are cut straight from the hip to add the extra fullness for the "gathered" effect and allow more than enough room to slide over the hips (A).

Combine this with a too-crisp or too-heavy fabric and the result is a lumpy waistline. Be sure to check the suggested fabric on the pattern envelope to eliminate this problem, keeping in mind soft, drapey fabrics and light- to medium-weight knits are the best choices for this cut.

Styles designed with a separate waistband for the elastic are a nice alternative to the traditional fold-down casing (B).

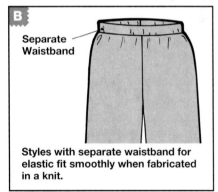

Separate Waistband

Styles with separate waistband for elastic fit smoothly when fabricated in a knit.

This design is best for knits, because the pants or skirt can be fit fairly smoothly over the hip and waist, yet retain enough stretch to pull up easily over the hips. That means less fullness—and therefore less lumpiness—all the way around the waistband.

To keep elastic smooth and wrinkle-free inside a casing or waistband, try these tricks:

✂ Turn and press the casing or apply the waistband for the elastic, then edgestitch the upper fold (C).

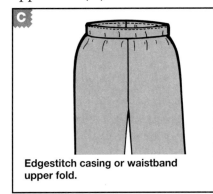

Edgestitch casing or waistband upper fold.

✂ Insert the elastic and complete the casing or waistband. Try on the pants or skirt and adjust the fullness evenly, inserting a pin through the casing or waistband and the elastic at the center front and back and each side seam. *Note:* If your pant pattern has no side seams, position the pins halfway between the center front and back seams.

✂ Remove the garment and stitch through the casing or waistband and elastic at each pin mark (D). The elastic will stay flat inside the casing and the fullness won't migrate and bunch up in one place.

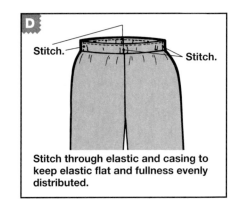

Stitch.   Stitch.

Stitch through elastic and casing to keep elastic flat and fullness evenly distributed.

150

Q **Because my waist is larger than average for my hip size, I'm most comfortable in dresses with elasticized waistlines. How can I add an elasticized waistline to a dress designed with a normal waistline?**

A To change a fitted waistline to an elasticized one, follow these easy steps:

✂ Eliminate any waistline darts or tucks in the bodice. If there are no darts in the existing pattern but the side seams angle in at the waistline edge, cut the bodice straight down from the armhole (A, page 133).

✂ If the skirt has darts, eliminate them.

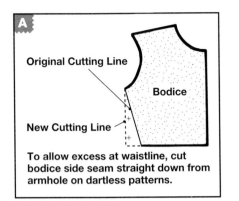

To allow excess at waistline, cut bodice side seam straight down from armhole on dartless patterns.

✄ For maximum waistline comfort and a smooth, non-roll elastic application, use 1"-wide nylon mesh elastic. To compensate for the wide elastic, you'll need to add extra room in the waistline seam allowance: For 1"-wide elastic, cut the bodice and skirt with 1½"-wide waistline seam allowances (B).

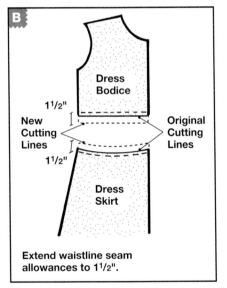

Extend waistline seam allowances to 1½".

✄ Easestitch the skirt waistline 1½" and again 1¼" from the raw edge (C). Pin the skirt to the bodice, drawing up the easestitching to fit the bodice waistline.

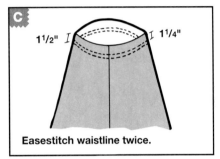

Easestitch waistline twice.

✄ Stitch 1½" from the skirt/bodice raw edges. Press the seam toward the bodice and stitch through all layers 1¼" from the waistline seamline, leaving a 2" to 3" opening for threading the elastic (D, page 134).

D

2" To 3" Elastic Opening

1¹/₂"   1¹/₄"

I 1¹/₄"

Stitch 1¹/₂" from raw edges and
press seam toward bodice; stitch
through all layers 1¹/₄" from
waistline seam.

✂ Cut enough 1"-wide elastic for a comfortable fit, plus 1" for overlap, and thread it through the waistline. Temporarily pin the elastic ends with a safety pin, then try on the garment and adjust the waistline fit as needed. Overlap the elastic ends and stitch them securely.

✂ Complete the waistline casing stitching.

INDEX